"This is a fascinating work. Eloise Ristad discusses the problems of nervousness and/or nervous energy with a physiological understanding of human behavior under stress, imaginative and original psychological insight, and just plain good common sense. The valuable solutions she suggests for the problems of musical performance can be applied just as readily to the vast gamut of physical and intellectual actions and reactions any individual is confronted with in daily living."
—**Samuel Sanders,** concert pianist, professor, Juilliard School of Music.

"This book turns traditional music teaching on its head. Control by letting go—excellence by not trying—learning by simple awareness. The principles are true; their expression lyrical, readable, and helpful."
—**Timothy Gallwey,** author of *The Inner Game of Tennis.*

"It moves me deeply. I sang through it, I danced through it, I laughed through it. It is the natural, universal way of growing and learning. You said it all. It was like a rush of all I have done and felt and wanted to do with my students—young and old. You have put sense into the years of my teaching." —**Mona Dayton,** National Teacher of the Year, 1966, and professor emerita, Long Island University.

"There are many ingenious and useful ideas here for teachers, learners, or makers of music." —**John Holt,** author of *How Children Fail, How Children Learn,* and other books about learning and education.

"How grateful I am to Eloise Ristad! She could have used lots of heavy-duty '-ology' words to tell us what she's learned—the message is valid and profound—but she chooses to invite us to a party instead of a lecture. It's only later, with the smile still on your face, that you realize how much good the book has done for you as well."
—**Denise McCluggage,** author of *The Centered Skier.*

"This is a gem of a book for all students and teachers of life-learning. May the joy and fun of learning dance on forever!" —**Al Chung-liang Huang,** T'ai Chi master and author of *Embrace Tiger, Return to Mountain* and *Tao: The Watercourse Way.*

"Eloise Ristad brings playfulness back into playing the piano, the flute, clarinet, drums or vocal chords. Yet musicians aren't the only ones who will discover something new and refreshing in this book, for what she writes of her experiments and observations has to do with life itself." —**Barry Stevens,** author of *Don't Push the River* and *Person to Person.*

"Eloise Ristad emerges as a gifted writer as well as musician and teacher. The book is a pleasure to read and an adventure in achieving the kind of inner freedom everyone longs for. We see objectified with great wit those authority figures who have unwittingly deprived us of our inner freedom. Without that freedom, there is no center out of which to speak, to sing, to dance, to make music, to live. I confidently predict a wide appeal, and not by any means only to musicians." —**Gladys Weibel Goldman,** Librarian for English and American Literature, emerita, University of Colorado at Boulder.

"Eloise Ristad is a splendid musician and one of the best, and most successful, teachers I've met. I predict that few will come away from her book unchanged. Although she is writing specifically about music, she is really writing more generally about human beings who are involved in, and excited about, learning something important to them." —**Tony Kallet,** Ph.D. psychology, musician, editor of *OUTLOOK.*

"As a professional dancer and singer, it is indeed encouraging to see these important concepts so clearly and passionately articulated. I was particularly interested in the universal meaning and cross-disciplinary application of concepts that are crucial to unlocking and freeing the creative process—a wonderful guide for all of us, musicians as well as non-musicians." —**Paul Oertel,** Nancy Spanier Dance Theatre.

"Wonderfully refreshing, honest and clear, this is a life-affirming book with tremendous practical value. In one chapter, for instance, Eloise Ristad addresses the would-be pianist in a way that demystifies—in utmost simplicity—the whole process of reading music. Throughout, she speaks directly to the musician and the performer in each of us, encouraging us to celebrate the authenticity of our inner wisdom and to discover our wholeness. It's about time this book was written!" —**Virginia Veach,** Ph.D., therapist.

Dedicated to Millie and Bill Stein, my ninety-one-year-old parents, who have followed the progress of my work and my writing with keen interest, even to the point of participating in one of my upside-down workshop sessions.

A Soprano on Her Head

By Eloise Ristad

Right-side-up reflections on life and other performances

Art direction; cover and graphic design—Roberta Haldeman
and Ed Huston

Cover Art—Ed Huston
Line drawings—Millie Pendergast

Copyright © 1982 by Eloise Ristad
Real People Press
Box F
Moab, Utah, 84532

ISBN: 0-911226-20-6 clothbound $10.00
ISBN: 0-911226-21-4 paperbound $6.50

Library of Congress Cataloging in Publication Data:

Ristad, Eloise.
    A soprano on her head.

    1. Music—Instruction and study.   I. Title.
MT2.R57   780'.7   81-23369
ISBN 0-911226-20-6   AACR2
ISBN 0-911226-21-4 (pbk.)

3   4   5   6   7   8   9   10   Printing   89   88   87

Acknowledgements

It all began at Kendra's. I had fantasized earlier that summer about getting away to "some place near ocean and mountains" to write. It's so easy to dream there's a book in your head when new insights and ideas begin tickling the inside of your brain. Then Kendra Sherritt, a former piano student, called, offering me her home in Santa Barbara for an entire month. Ocean, mountains, time, a house to myself, a typewriter, piano and car—there were no excuses left.

I wrote. Eight chapters of rough draft and back home again, I discovered how many of my friends were proficient editors, ready and willing to lend their help. The book is a celebration of support and encouragement from friends, colleagues, family, students and workshop participants who cheered me on both in my work and in my writing. Although writing a book can be a lonely task, it was rarely so in this case, for someone was always waiting for the next installment.

There was Howie, for instance—Howard Movshovitz, film critic, friend, and English teacher, who believed in the book and believed in me from the first tentative version to the last draft. Disconcertingly honest, he never restrained his response, whether it happened to be a growl over lack of clarity or a "Whew!" when my writing struck a deep chord. How many hours of editing help he contributed!

Mary McDermott Shideler, theologian, author and current president of The Society for Descriptive Psychology, offered not only her enthusiastic support and help but also a haven at her magnificent home in the mountains whenever I needed inspiration. At a crucial point in the writing, I met Brian Brooks, poet, journalist and therapist, who fell in love with the book. Brian became so attuned to the rhythm of my writing that he gave me no peace when he sensed I had lost that rhythm. Tony Kallet, editor of *Outlook* magazine, psychologist, and fellow musician, read the manuscript with a special ear for style and content. Leslie Hyde, budding young writer and friend, took great delight—as I did—in our many sessions together over the manuscript. The sparks flew from the words and phrases that collided in mid-air as we searched for more appropriate imagery for certain uncooperative passages. Several of my children got in the act from time to time with similar help.

So many more. There were people like Lorin Hollander and Larry Graham, concert pianists, and Paul Oertel, professional dancer, urging me on. There were colleagues and friends—musical and otherwise— such as Lois Sollenberger, David Goldberg, Cheryl Bailey, Dorothy Satten, Forrest Williams, Norma Register, Linda Jones, Virginia Sutton, and Gladys Weibel Goldman, who gave valuable comments and editing suggestions on certain chapters. The list could go on, for people kept popping up who wanted to read some of the manuscript and who always contributed in some way. Bobi Haldeman, who later poured her heart into art direction, read the first draft of Chapter One and announced, "I know what the title should be: *A Soprano on Her Head!"* Of course. Why hadn't I known that? When I was searching for a subtitle, another friend, Marilyn Pitcairn, sparked the idea for "right-side-up reflections." Millie Pendergast started out typing manuscript, and responded to what she was typing by sketching characters that later found their way into the chapter headings. Ed Huston spent untold hours absorbing ideas from the book before he picked up his paint brush to work on the cover.

My husband Adam, read proof with a keen eye, critiqued, and constantly shared my excitement about new insights. And throughout, students and workshop participants explored new territory with varying amounts of curiosity, resistance and enthusiasm, furnishing much of the material for the book.

And at the end, Steve and Connirae Andreas did the important job of final editing, conscientiously alert not only to necessary changes but also to their wish not to edit me out of my writing. In addition they allowed me the unheard-of privilege and delight of participating in all artistic decisions concerning the book.

I extend my appreciation and grateful acknowledgment to all— named and unnamed—who are so much a part of this adventure in writing.

Eloise Ristad

Contents

11. Maybe I Should Just Keep Bees!

Many of us are ensnared in a debilitating "super-person" act as we try conscientiously to live up to unreal expectations and demands. What luxury to know we can permit ourselves to be human, and that being human means that we may even "fail" at some of the preposterous goals we set for ourselves. Once we abandon our overearnest trying, we often find ourselves closer to our real goals.

12. Maybe I Like My Problems

Problems, unfortunately, can sometimes be addictive. The very familiarity of the struggle offers reassurance, whether the struggle is in cleaning up a Brahms Rhapsody at the piano or in solving problems in a relationship. If we can give up our addiction long enough to fully imagine ourselves without the problem, we can often step confidently onto new ground, ready to explore.

13. Clammy Hands and Shaky Knees

What are your own symptoms of stage fright? Do you mask the actual physical sensations under the unspecific label of "nervousness?" If you are willing to go beyond the label and explore your stage fright through a variety of topsy-turvy approaches, your shaky knees might even learn how to behave.

14. "So You Were a Flop!"

What devastating words to hear, yet at the same time how comforting to hear someone say them out loud. When we stop our pretending and say such words aloud to ourselves, we sometimes discover new strengths.

15. "Who Me? Did I Play That?"

Once we drop our preoccupation with the "right way," improvising freely with movement or music can provide us with a metaphor for improvising in our lives. The freedom we gain can take us beyond the narrow boundaries of our existence and introduce us to lively characters within us waiting to emerge. These new characters enrich our performances, on or off stage.

16. Soprano on Her Feet

A soprano can't really build a career standing on her head. Preposterous, fascinating experiments must ultimately lead us back to singing on our feet, or playing the piano in a bow tie. If the soprano takes singing on her head as a new formula for success, she will be disappointed. If she takes each successful experiment as a literal solution to her problems, she misses the point. Often in life we must stand on our heads before we can come full circle and turn ourselves right-side-up once again.

Afterword

Foreword

Eloise Ristad deals here with complex problems which torment and cripple so many of our most creative and talented people, and she does so with compassion, wisdom, and wit. The problem of stage fright, for instance, is a suffering of epidemic proportions in our society, and involves modalities of thought and projections that rob spontaneity and enthusiasm in artistic performance.

Those interested in creative education have long felt that an entirely new, holistic and nurturing process of allowing individuals to discover and express themselves is needed if our educational system is to avoid the neuroses and creative blocks of the past generation. This book illuminates through its conversational style the destructive inhibitions, fears, and guilt experienced by all of us as we fail to break through to creativity. This story is told to me day after day in conservatories and college campuses around the world. Indeed I felt at times that she was telling of my own most petty and debilitating fears.

But what is important, *A Soprano on Her Head* supplies answers and methods for overcoming these universal psychological blocks— methods that have not only been proven in her own studio, but which trace back through history to the oldest and wisest systems of under-standing the integration of mind and body. The work bears scrutiny both scientifically and holistically.

This is a wonderful book. Read it. You are not alone.

Lorin Hollander, concert pianist.

Introduction

A friend offered me the use of his mountain hideout one August. He gave me three keys to use: one for the cabin and one for each of two gates on the dirt road to the cabin. The first gate was open so I drove through. The second was locked, but none of the three keys worked. *Wrong gate, maybe. Did Dale give me the right keys?* It was fifty miles back to the city. *Ah, there's another padlock. Stupid of me not to notice.* I tried the keys again. Nothing budged. *Hey! A third padlock. Whew!* The first key didn't fit. *Next one, maybe.* No. *The third one has to do it.*

By the time I found the fourth padlock I was nearly in tears. I had already taken three wrong turns up the mountain, mistaking driveways to hidden cabins for the main road that meandered sloppily here and there. Now an ordinary gate had turned vicious and blocked my way. Before I even tried, I knew no key would budge this last lock. Two keys fit perfectly but wouldn't turn.

I sat down on a rock to pull my jumbled thoughts together. *These have to be the right keys; this has to be the right gate. You're just getting spooked because the sun is almost down and everything is unfamiliar.* I took a deep breath. *Easy now. Start once more with the first lock. Be sure to try each key. Don't mix up the two that look alike.*

It worked. The first, most visible padlock yielded easily to the second key. I looked over my shoulder to be sure no one was watching this ridiculous drama. Impersonal boulders and pine trees stared back, mocking me.

The next fiasco involved carefully taking the first right turn beyond the gate, which took me to the wrong cabin at the end of the road. I re-read my directions—they were clear enough—and backed down the narrow, rutted, twisting road. I parked the car and took two more wrong roads on foot. *Maybe he meant first left instead of right, or maybe the second turn to the right? . . .* I felt as though I were searching for a cabin that surely didn't exist. Finally I took off through the woods, knowing that cabins don't dematerialize. Suddenly, there it was. I followed the driveway out, found my car and realized that my friend had indeed goofed on the directions. He *had* meant the first turn to the left, but unfortunately the first turn to the left didn't look like a road until well past the first overgrown curve.

In my yellow-grey-green frustration I knew there was some kind of emotional overload that had to do with more than padlocked gates, unidentifiable roads, and disappearing cabins. After I built a fire in my elusive cabin, I curled up on a low stool, hugged my knees and contemplated. How many times in my life had soap-opera drama presented seemingly unconquerable barriers? I thought of the long search for right keys in a first marriage—of the inevitable struggle with locks and keys in raising children.

I had escaped to my friend's cabin that month to work on this book. How familiar these frustrations and releases felt—how symbolic of what I feel in my writing, in my teaching, in my life. As I sat there, I thought about how often we put right keys into wrong locks, and wrong keys into right locks, and right keys into right locks without knowing about the slight twist to the left before the turn to the right. I was reminded of times when I've followed the advice of an "expert" who supposedly knows the way, only to find that the directions are garbled, or that they work for the expert but not for me, and I have to find my own path through the woods. I thought about my own work with performers in workshops entitled "The Performer Within," for it was from these sessions that I was drawing much of the material for my writing. I realized that what excited me most in these workshops was the fun of tracking down the subtle twists and turns that can lead to more comfortable learning or performing. These discoveries always feel like keys that coax open resistant locks.

I usually recommend that participants in my workshops read such books as *The Inner Game of Tennis* by Timothy Gallwey and *The Centered Skier* by Denise McCluggage. These particular books do a splendid job of attuning people ahead of time to the principles of awareness, curiosity and imagery that are so effective in tricking our inner judges out of the way. Once we have sent our judges packing for the moment, we are free to do some upside-down experimenting that can lead to some right-side-up solutions.

Over and over I find that such approaches bring about astonishing changes, just as similar approaches work their magic on the tennis court or the ski slope. The drama in the immediate results can be misleading, however, so read the book with some skepticism as well as openness. Your skepticism will protect you from accepting the results at face value without a deeper understanding of the profound underlying principles. This book is not intended as a manual of easy answers, despite the many accounts of deceptively simple solutions to familiar problems. Things are not as easy as they seem. My soprano, for instance, got turned upside-down in the course of her frustration, and went from welcome release upside-down to more frustration before she could sing again right-side-up. So it was on the mountainside; so it is in life as well. Yet if we are willing to abandon our usual coercive tactics and approach our problems sideways and kitty-corner we stand a good chance of finding our way through some interesting gates.

Although connecting threads weave their way through the entire book, most chapters are complete in themselves. Read them as you wish, in whichever order. For just as you will find no "right" answers in this book, you will find no "right" order to these reflections and musings and explorations. I would like to be able to design the table of contents in a circle, or in some kind of overlapping collage, with unnumbered chapter headings.

When I first discovered I had a book that wanted writing, I set out to write for musicians. Yet just as tennis and skiing provide the performer with useful metaphors, I found the insights gained in my workshops for musicians expanding into metaphors for life in general. Life in turn provided metaphors for the musician. As I wrote, I found myself speaking not only to musicians but to non-musicians as well, to would-be musicians and to almost musicians who had had a go at lessons when they were younger, to dancers and actors on the stage and to those who dance and act their way through life. Music being the way it is, my writing got all mixed up with such things as ski lessons and hiking, with bee-keeping and knuckle-rapping, with right brains and left brains and no brains and jumbled brains, and—with a soprano on her head.

1. Meet the Soprano

"How long have you been enlightened?" The question startled me, and I laughed it off with "It's craziness, not enlightenment."

"No, I'm serious," pursued Liz, who had just discovered the craziest of all ways to decrescendo her big operatic voice to a whisper. The non-traditional workshops that I lead for musicians usually start with body movement warm-ups that are designed to encourage spontaneity. The effect is both exhilarating and exhausting. After one such warm-up all eight of us in that particular group stretched out on the floor, sensing our bodies, our breath, and then our voices, until we found the most comfortable tones we could produce. As we let the tones change and followed the changes with body movement, Liz, our soprano, ended up on her knees with her head upside down on the floor.

Effortlessly, and without thinking how—for who could have told her how to sing on her head—she found all the resonance she had been struggling for, with the added bonus of incredible dynamic control. The rest of us had goose bumps and shivers as we listened to her voice fade in and out. Someone went to the piano and started the Mozart aria that Liz had been singing earlier, just to see if standing on her head would work as well for Mozart as it had with random tones. It did, and our goose bumps got bumpier.

"I love it, I love it! It feels wonderful!" said Liz as she sat up and let the blood run back where it belonged.

I jokingly promised to compose a piece for a soprano on her head, if we could figure out which way a soprano on her head should face.

"Try it standing up now, but close your eyes as you sing and imagine you are on your head with all that natural resonance available." She tried, and though there was certainly some improvement over her earlier effort, she still felt the familiar clutch when she was in the usual

5

standing position. All her years of conditioning—her years of passively accepting vocal "prescriptions"—were not to be discarded so easily. She was once again trying as hard as she could to make it work, to *make* it sound like it had when she was on her head.

"Okay, this time don't pay any attention to how it sounds. Just sense how your knees feel. Sense your forehead, the back of your neck, your feet."

Since she didn't know how her knees *ought* to feel, she just sensed them. Next I asked her to touch different parts of her body as she continued to sing, without worrying about how she produced the tone. She bent over to touch her legs and knees, straightened up with a long, leisurely movement, stroked the back of her head, then reached an arm out and with the other hand brushed it lightly from her fingertips all the long way up to her shoulder. She then stroked the other arm, slowly, with sensuous movements that involved her whole body, singing all the while.

The goose bumps came back as we heard the tone change. Liz approached the high note that always produced the biggest clutch and sailed into it effortlessly.

"I can't believe it. I really cannot believe what's happening," she broke off in the middle of the next phrase.

The ingredients for such small miracles are simple. First, like Liz, a person must accept permission to be free of the usual restrictions. Each of us is partly a childlike, unselfconscious being who can stay in the present moment without thinking of the millions of other moments in our lives. My job is not only to give a person permission to discover moment-by-moment awareness; it is to create a climate in which that person can give herself that permission. From there on it is just a matter of designing experiments to trick our old stuffy "know-it-all" chattering self out of the way. If a person is as ready for change as Liz, the results can be dramatic.

Liz had come to the six-day workshop baffled by the title "The Performer Within," but curious. A superb public school music teacher, she had experienced some crises in her personal life that led from frustration and hurt to some new growing and unfolding. Now she was almost brave enough to leave her old job and try out her big, wonderful voice on stage. Ready, that is, if she could only solve some of her old tension problems that plagued her when she even thought about performing. Since traditional voice instruction only increased that tension, she was more than ready to experiment. With such openness it was easy for her to let her body become a voice, the voice become movement, and so on, until she ended up on her head singing Mozart.

Do the discoveries made with Liz mean that standing on your head is a "new method" of voice instruction? Is it a marvelous new approach which will solve every singer's problems?

Of course not. As we experimented, we happened to stumble onto something that worked remarkably well for Liz, and which might indeed work for another singer as well. (It worked no magic for my voice, unfortunately!) In the course of the next few days we stumbled onto some entirely different ideas, some of which worked remarkably well for other members of the group, some of which did not. The important thing we did was to establish an open, flexible, experimental state of mind—a state of curiosity and excitement.

Without the kind of excitement Liz had about change, people will gain little in such a group. Jack, for instance, went to great lengths explaining how difficult it was for him to play slow music. He played an adagio movement from a Beethoven piano sonata, and sure enough, he had trouble playing slow music. There was no substance or depth to the music. That puzzled me, for I sensed that he was sensitive and intuitive. As we worked to increase his awareness of the expressive qualities of the music, he would seem on the edge of a breakthrough, but would then back off and happily return to "having trouble playing slow music." Each time change threatened, something in him would push the barriers back in place. It became apparent that his need to prove his original statement was more important to him than the need for change.

On the last day of the workshop, he brought some yellowed sheet music to class. It was a set of Moravian dances, written in an improvisatory manner, full of lush romantic nuances. We were surprised when he played these with all the sensitivity and warmth that had been missing before. We were less puzzled when we learned that he had grown up in a Moravian family, and that these dances were part of his heritage—something he felt in the marrow of his bones. He had danced to this kind of music countless times as a child, but in his adult life he had tucked away the bone feelings and the muscle memory of joyous movement. He had put a part of himself "on hold"—a part that was reluctant to be discovered and that scurried into its hole as soon as we got back to Beethoven.

A woman in the same group struck me as another person who would be resistant to change. Jane seemed a trifle too proper and too well-organized to respond with spontaneity in such an unconventional workshop. I knew before she sat down that first day that dust would avoid her windowsill and settle on mine. I suspected that she would never be late for an appointment, and that her playing would be enviably accurate. I also guessed that she would be put off by the warm-ups, so I was delighted when she proved me wrong by wholeheartedly participating. When it was her turn to play she went to the piano eagerly—as curious as a puppy meeting a turtle—and played the first movement of a Mozart sonata.

My first flash of intuition about her playing had been right. It was brilliant and so accurate that it was hard to pin down what it needed. I stalled for time a bit, then plunged in and asked her to play a certain passage from the exposition of the sonata. Again we heard the well-practiced, meticulous sound, a close replica of the first time.

I knew then what I wanted to try. "Jane, could you play that passage in an ugly way?" She was hesitant, but game, and tried for "ugliness." . . .

"Okay, now play it like a tragic, slow movement." Someone in the group threw in "frivolous," someone else "pathetic," and another "lighthearted." . . .

"Now just go back and find out how the passage plays itself, without any directing from your brain," I said.

"You know," responded Jane when she finished, "that's interesting. I liked it much better that time than I ever have before, yet I can't pin down what happened. It's as though each way I played it had something to offer, even when I tried to make it ugly. Then when I let go of all my expectations and simply let my fingers play it, it was somehow fresher and more exciting."

She was right. The passage now had subtleties that could never have been planned. We are so easily trapped by the all-too-common assumption that a composer can actually indicate the wide range of dynamic nuances necessary in a piece of music with his use of squared-off symbols such as *p, f, mp, mf,* or even ⟍⟍⟍ and ⟋⟋⟋ . These symbols indicate only on a gross level that the composer wants a passage soft, loud, moderately soft, moderately loud, or that he wants a gradual crescendo from soft to loud or a decrescendo from loud to soft. But careful following of these signs will not blow the spark of life into the music. By experimenting with the terms "ugly," "frivolous," and "pathetic," she bypassed her usual responses to symbols and discovered the qualities in the music that had prompted the symbols.

At the next session we worked with another section of her sonata that had a shallow kind of brilliance. I asked Jane to leave the piano bench and show us her concept of the passage in body movement. This was new to her. She was accustomed to putting her brain in "overdrive" when she practiced, which meant that her body got left out of the process—unless it screamed in pain when she overdid things. She was selfconscious at first, but soon got caught up in experimenting and began to feel the vitality of the passage in her body.

Back at the piano, she played the passage while the rest of us danced to it. "The way you play it will choreograph our movement" I told her. The vitality she had experienced in her body transferred into the music before she had a chance to put her brain to work. Again Jane was delighted.

She came back to the next class with aching muscles, and could hardly wait to describe where her experimenting had taken her at home. She had disrupted the usual orderliness of her living room by moving every loose piece of furniture out of her way so she could have more space to try out her pieces in body movement, while her startled family had watched with no small amount of puzzlement. Their puzzlement increased as they heard strange and unfamiliar sounds at the piano.

I had not expected this kind of involvement from Jane when I had first sensed her need for order and perfection. But she had been through a difficult period in her life when her perfectionism had led to serious problems. Fortunately, she had found a therapist who was helping her go beyond the rigid set of rules that had previously formed her boundaries. The workshop served as a kind of celebration of her life-energy, a rediscovery of childlike (not childish) enthusiasm.

At times Jane would cling to a specific remedy which had worked particularly well in freeing her in her playing. But she realized rather quickly that the remedy was not as important as an open experimental state of mind that allowed for some possible failures along the way. She coveted speed in her playing, but since she felt that speed and accuracy thumb their noses at each other, she ordinarily opted for caution. I suggested that she just *pretend* she could play faster, and not worry about the wrong notes she might play.

"How remarkable," she said at the end of a page played with a new sense of reckless abandon. "I took you quite literally and really stopped fretting about mistakes. I thought it would be fun for once, even if it was a mess. But it wasn't a mess, was it?"

It most certainly was not.

Jane had worked long and hard for accuracy and did not want to lose it; she also knew she felt cheated when people commented in awe "Don't you *ever* make any mistakes?" She felt the music so deeply that she wanted much more than accuracy. She wanted excitement and depth. She welcomed anything that would help her dump her *addiction* to accuracy without upsetting the accuracy itself. When she found herself playing with new excitement without sacrificing her clean technique, she was elated.

We tell ourselves so many lies and half-truths. "I can't play *that* fast. I can't play slow music well. I can't hit that high note without clutching. I can't memorize well. I'm a lousy sight-reader. This passage is going too well—I'll probably blow it. Oops, here comes that spot—I'll never make it through. Everyone else can play more difficult music than I can. I'm just a phony who has bluffed my way to the top and they'll find me out."

We listen and are duly impressed and intimidated by these inner voices that turn into unseen judges that nag at us. We give each of these judges a seat of honor in our minds, all the while hating their guts and their never-ending supply of judgments. As we practice, one part of us glances nervously over our shoulder, wondering if we are doing it "right." "Am I doing good?" a talented young eight-year-old student wrote in my Christmas card once, giving me shivers of doubt about my teaching process.

If we teach, we feel the sodden breath of our judges reminding us that we could have done a better job, that we haven't really given the student his money's worth today, that we haven't covered what the pedagogy course outlined, that other teachers must surely pack more into each hour of teaching. When we taste victory in a fine performance, our judges immediately set up expectations for the next performance, which must be still better.

It is as though we insert the judges between ourselves and our experience, which is like making love with our clothes on, missing the skin-to-skin, body-to-body immediacy of full contact. We give the judges permission to accompany us on each journey of life, never daring to realize that we can park them, at least momentarily.

In the middle of her wonderful experiments, Liz, the soprano, lapsed into her usual overdeveloped conscientiousness about "how to do it" without even realizing it. "Darn," she said, snapping her fingers, "I *know* I should be making my pelvis solid as a rock to give some support to the tone."

"Should?" we all echoed, incredulous, for she had been so delighted to chuck the "shoulds." She shook her head and grinned, recognizing how easily she had trapped herself.

"Let your pelvis melt; let it do anything. I don't care what. Just sense it and find out how it feels when you are singing. And let the tone be good, bad, or whatever."

The tone, of course, soared up and out of a pelvis that was free to feel, and therefore free to release energy into the tone.

2. The Book of Judges

By sensing her pelvis, Liz tricked her judges out of the way long enough to produce a rich vocal tone. In workshops we not only trick judges, but also confront them. We often visualize judges in a circle about us and give them shape and form. For some, the judges are dark blobs of discomfort; for others, they are human, recognizable personalities, often appearing as parents or other authority figures from the past.

If we stand in the center of our circle, we can look around at each judge with a sense of detachment and curiosity and find out what each one is telling us. We can also take the initiative and talk back to them; we can ask them to be more supportive and to stop tyrannizing us. We can let their cold imperiousness turn the judges into ice, then let a tiny warm glow at our center intensify little by little until our judges begin to melt away. After experimenting with such imagery, one workshop participant found his judges trickling down a rocky slope and into a rushing stream.

In one session, a young woman giggled out loud as her judges—all of them familiar characters from her everyday life—grew long noses. In the next session we used her image, but first dressed our judges in long, dignified robes. As we imagined them growing long noses, we also stripped them of their robes and watched them scurry for cover, completely naked. As we laughed them away we realized that they had lost some of their power.

We *can* lessen the power of these nagging, bothersome judges that continually defeat us and stifle our spontaneity. We aren't doomed to constant censorship from these commentators on our every act and thought. There is even a chance that we can come to terms with them and find the good in them.

Experiment for a moment. Close your eyes and look at your own private collection of judges. You will find these shadowy characters rather easily. They are the figures of authority who impose heavy rules upon you—who send you off on endless missions of duty rather than let you know what you really want and need. They are the ones you keep trying to shove out of the ragged edge of your consciousness, but that hang on with the obstinacy of spoiled children. They are the ones who give you that vaguely uncomfortable feeling in your gut when you don't measure up to their invisible yardstick, when you have been a little too ridiculous, or when you have had some delightfully wicked fantasy. They are the creatures looming, dark and ominous, when you know you are much less good than your public self seems.

Let your judges take the form they wish. Most of us have instant access to these murky figures who are such dedicated companions. Gather your judges together. Jerk the smug one out from behind your right shoulder, grab the condescending one from behind your left shoulder, and see if one is menacing you from above. Put them all out in front of you with a firm hand and look. Just look.

As you look, sense the power these judges wield. Feel their effects in your gut, in your chest, in your forehead, in your jaw. Notice where your tongue is pressing. Don't try to relax—just sense, physically and emotionally, the power of these judges.

Let yourself become thoroughly familiar with the sensations you feel. These sensations will become a future reference point, so let yourself be curious about them. You've often gone to great lengths to escape these feelings; now your task is to find out all you can about them.

When you have sensed the nature of your judges as fully as you can, leave them for a moment. Breathe a small pinpoint of light or energy into your center. . . . Let each breath intensify that energy. . . . Slowly let yourself expand with each breath, with each small fanning of that inward energy. . . . Feel energy flow down from your center through your pelvis, your thighs, your knees, lower legs, your ankles, into your heels and feet, all the way to the ends of your toes. . . . Feel your connection with the ground—with the support beneath your feet. . . . Feel energy surge upwards from your center, filling your chest, your neck, up through the top of your head, through your arms and wrists and fingers. . . . Let yourself change from small and vulnerable to expanding and powerful. . . . Sense your body, sense your breathing, sense your *self* and revel in the intensity of the sensations.

Now come back to your judges. Look at them carefully again. Keep sensing your body, your breathing, the sense of power that you have. Don't *try* to feel powerful, just tune in to whatever sense of power is there.

Do your judges wear the faces of people from your everyday life? Of your parents? Teachers? Priest? Rabbi? Guru? Do the faces melt together into your own disapproving face and consciousness? Find out. Go along with your perceptions, and continue to feel your own power center, your own sense of being, your right to be totally you and no other. As you sense yourself more deeply, you can afford to reach out to your judges. Have a dialogue with them. Let them speak their piece about what they expect you to be, and answer clearly that you are only who you are. Ask them for support of whoever you happen to be. Ask them to pack all of their expectations back into their traveling bags.

Now feel your goodness, your badness; your kindness, your meanness; your strength, your weakness; your talents, your un-talents; your dedication, your laziness. Feel all the opposites that comprise your being human. Feel the power in these opposing forces within you. Without these opposites you would be as bland and characterless as unsalted mush.

Feel how that power in your opposites reduces your judges to caricatures. Let those judges put on a show now—poking their fingers at you, jumping up and down with their silly demands, unrolling endless scrolls with their impossible list of expectations. Listen to them chatter and yammer at you. Pay attention to the tone of voice they use as they call your name over and over. Jonathon, *Jon*athon . . . *Jonathon, Jonathon, Jonathon.* . . . Stay with one of those voices and identify it so you will recognize it the next time it tries to intrude. Hear your first and last name—*Jonathon BROWN*—and see how that adds to the sense of demand. Add your middle name—*Jonathon ANTHONY Brown*—and it may add even more urgency.

Now let the voice change to cartoon character pitch. Let it change to the sound of a mosquito buzzing around your head. Add the rest of your judges until you have a whole swarm of mosquitoes. Turn your imagination loose with any image that joggles your funny bone, and when you have had enough, order them to leave, or zap them all with judge dissolver.

Take a deep breath and enjoy the instant of respite. When the judges come back, see if they have changed; see if they are a little confused or a little quieter. Look at each of them with understanding, as you would any pathetic, unreasonable character. Even love them a little, because like it or not, they are parts of you, and they really do mean well. But no thanks, you aren't buying any garbage today. They may well catch you unawares another time, but for now, this moment, you know their game. Then tell them to run along, because right now you are too busy being you to bother with them. Watch your judges—seedy characters that they are—pack their peddler's bags, and wave them off once again.

Flip back for an instant to sensing the tyranny of your judges—to that jagged discomfort. And then return, either to your amused tolerance for your judges' antics, or to the strength in your honest anger. Find out how it feels to travel back and forth, so you can clearly recognize each state. Let your sense of humor be triggered the next time you are practicing for a concert and recognize a whack from your judges/persecutors. Be ready to respond with an "Aha, I caught you red-handed" when they slip back into being outrageous monitors of your existence.

Savor the instant of your "Aha," for that is the instant that you own your own power. It is the instant of transformation, for ownership denotes strength. The energy you have given your judges suddenly becomes available for solving problems, for practicing effectively for your concert. I once watched a woman grab a bataca in a psychodrama session and own her outdated rage at her father. Her exhaustion was transformed into energy as she used the bataca to beat on an empty chair representing him. As we own our rage at our judges, we also own the energy that it takes to suppress that rage. When the woman had spent her rage on her empty-chair/father, she was free to own the good feelings trickling in to fill up the emptied-out space. When we have spent our rage at our judges, we free them to become non-judgmental guides.

Once we have stripped our judges of their crippling power over us, they can become positive voices, advising us in a friendly way, giving us accurate information when we need it. They can become the common sense part that says "Hey, wait a minute," before we plunge into one more overburdening good cause, before we stumble into some crazy-making situation, before we let ourselves get caught in one more ego trap.

When I listen only to the nagging, worrisome level of what the judges are saying, I get the message that I ought to be doing a million things that are necessary, worthy, and of the utmost importance. When I pin one of these judges down and ask him directly what he has to offer me, I get a straighter message. I discover that he wants me to accomplish things that are worthwhile and satisfying. I find that the discomfort I feel comes not just from what I am *not* doing, but also from the fact that I am already scattering my efforts by trying to do too much. Whew! I can take this judge's hand in mine and know I have an ally. When the next person knocks on my door with a new way to save the world, I can say "No" with a clear conscience.

Jane, the perfectionist, came back for some extra work a year after her first workshop, caught in a typical dilemma with her judges. One of them had convinced her that she should take over the youth group in her church since there was no one else to do the job and the group would obviously fall apart if someone didn't take over, and how could she expect people to be there when her kids got old enough for the group, if she didn't do her share now? Another judge, just as vocal, told her that since she had just purchased a lovely new grand piano, she should justify her purchase by giving a recital on it. The battle between these judges locked her body into destructive tensions that adversely affected her practicing as well as her temperament.

When I asked Jane to check things out with her judges on a deeper level, she made some surprising discoveries. When given the chance, a voice she had ignored let her admit that she couldn't stand working with a bunch of boisterous teenagers. When she gave her youth-group judge a shove, he changed his tone of voice and reminded her of her cherished dream of starting a bell choir, a dream that had been percolating in the back of her head for a long time. Her judge further took on the role of advisor by suggesting that she chuck the youth-group responsibility, devote herself to her recital for the time being, and go ahead with the bell choir only when the timing felt right. This inner dialogue with her judges all took place within a few moments one day as she sat on the piano bench. She opened her eyes astonished that life was not as complicated as she thought. When she got home, she found that her recital judge also needed some dealing with. Within the week the nudge into doing an overly ambitious program softened into the knowledge that for the time being she only wanted to share her joy in her new piano with a few intimate friends, playing only the pieces that felt safe and comfortable.

It is tempting for us as performers to separate the judges from ourselves and put them out in the audience. In working with some conservatory students, I had them imagine walking out on stage for a performance and looking into the audience to find their judges. It wasn't hard. The judges took shape immediately for one student. He recognized the three instructors who were to hear his annual juries and who had the power to decree whether he could remain at the conservatory or be banished the following year.

A well-known concert pianist confided that he feels the judge in the form of the "Music Critic," who becomes an awesome presence in the audience. Though this pianist projects marvelous confidence when performing, he still imbues this critical presence with supernormal powers of knowing all things about all music. At times, the presence turns into his father, who reared his prodigy child with extraordinary wisdom combined with extraordinary impatience; he combined wonderful gentleness when his talented son played "well" with unwonderful rage when the phrasing was not "right."

A group of junior high school piano students in a performance class visualized their judges after one student in the group confessed to terror at playing for her peers. Kelly cast her fellow students as critics. She feared they would hear each flaw in her playing, and would dislike her for her incompetence. How can anyone perform well with so much at stake?

I asked Kelly and the other six students to close their eyes, then talked them through the process of visualizing their judges: the judges who came to performance class with them, who followed them down the hallway to math class, who went along to the basketball game and home again, and the ones who really ganged up on them during a recital.

"Picture them clearly and choose one who gives you a really rough time. Have a dialogue with that one. Describe how you feel. . . . Ask for some understanding about how tough it feels when your hands shake and your stomach does flips. . . . Ask for some sympathy, some relenting of that heavy censoring, of that voice telling you you aren't good enough." I kept guiding them with suggestions that seemed appropriate, then we opened our eyes and shared what had happened.

"Funny thing," said one of the kids. "All my judges seemed to be adults."

"Really? Mine too!" from another. Funny thing.

"The strangest thing happened: my judge turned into myself after I started talking to it." More astonishment from others who had had the same experience.

Kelly described an argument with her judge. "I pleaded with him to listen to me, and he finally said he would try to understand."

We went around the rest of the circle. Then I said "Kelly, why don't you play your Brahms now?" As an afterthought I added "By the way, how are you feeling?"

Kelly checked. "It's really strange. I don't feel scared anymore." The strength in her performance confirmed that.

Instant success? Only for the moment. Kelly came back the next week as tense as ever about the recital the following Sunday. I let her perform her Brahms Intermezzo without referring to the experience the previous Saturday. It was pretty bad. Her shoulders were locked somewhere up around her ears, her forehead was tight, her hands shook and were totally unresponsive to her impatient demands.

"That was awful," groaned Kelly.

"Kelly, do you remember what we did in class last Saturday?"

"Oh . . . yeah, I had forgotten about that."

"Let's try it again. See how quickly you can find your judge."

She closed her eyes . . . there was silence . . . then without prompting, Kelly opened her eyes and turned back to the piano and reclaimed her power.

Did it hold for her performance on Sunday? Partially. Enough for her to know that she had a powerful tool for future performances. Each time she performed after that, she had a further chance to explore and be curious about what her judges were doing to her. She could even afford to remember the devastating experience that had corroborated all the fears her judges had dumped on her. Several months before I knew her as a student, she had performed in the recital all music students have nightmares about. She was playing a Bach Invention— No. 7, I believe, which is such an easy piece to turn your fingers loose on. A sudden moment of panic: her brain asked her fingers what they were doing, but neither her brain nor her fingers knew, and neither could find out in time to keep her from fleeing the stage in tears, humiliated.

It took a year and a half of experimenting with judges and performances before Kelly had the experience of performing so well that "I didn't want yesterday to end, I was so happy." Will all her performances have this quality from now on? Probably not. But it's reassuring to know that we can learn to deal with our judges with increasing effectiveness.

Another student who has difficulty with judges recently competed in a concerto competition. Jennifer loves performing, but an audition or competition sets up a real life drama with our fantasized judges, and she knew she never played her best in such situations. Though she had worked with her judges as Kelly had, and could shrug off the results of most competitions—good or bad—she felt the stakes were particularly high in this one because winning meant the opportunity to play with an orchestra. She had competed two years in a row without winning, and this was her last chance before she graduated from high school.

The morning of the competition was not conducive to a rested, relaxed state, since Jennifer had to take college entrance examinations for five solid hours. By the time she came to the studio to warm up, she was exhausted and peevish. I was in a similar state; I had just returned from several days at a state music teachers' convention and had heard enough scared kids in competition to last a lifetime. I was nervous about accompanying Jennifer; my own judges were telling me I was so exhausted I might goof, throw her off, and ruin her chances. Jennifer was to play the last movement of the Grieg Concerto for the audition and could play it well. We knew, however, that the competition would be rough. I also knew that Jennifer sometimes over-practiced hard passages and lost the spontaneity that such passages need.

"Eloise, how can I make it more exciting?" she pleaded, wanting some last-minute magic as she warmed up at my studio.

"What do you mean, make it exciting? Grieg did that already! Play the opening as though you had never heard it, and don't try to make it exciting. Just listen to the excitement that *is* there." The sound of forced excitement for the benefit of the judges disappeared and there was a new shape to the opening. We tried a few other tricks, but I sensed that she had had an overdose of Grieg that week. So I sent her outside for a walk around the block in the October sunshine. "I want you to forget about Grieg. Just take a slow walk and come back and tell me anything you happened to see, hear or touch." Jennifer gave me an exasperated look, even though by now she was accustomed to such strange suggestions. When she dutifully walked out the door, I wondered if she would be back.

She returned with a relaxed grin on her face. She had crackled leaves under her feet. She had chuckled at a squirrel's antics and had reveled in the tingly, sun-charged breeze. She had sensed how her body moved through blue and gold and chrysanthemum-colored space . . . and she had forgotten about Grieg.

But now it was time to think about more than squirrels and fall flowers. "As you play this afternoon, keep as alive to the music as you did to your walk. You will find just as many new sounds and sensations to delight you." I knew that if Jennifer made new discoveries in the music, the audience and the judges would share them.

But it was not enough. I saw the tension jump back into her shoulders and lips. "Jennifer, I want you to put yourself far above the recital hall, and give yourself X-ray vision. I want you to look down and see yourself out in the foyer before your time to play. See yourself and all the other contestants as caricatures, all frightfully nervous little figures way down below, scurrying around in a panic. Watch one of these figures when it is time to play—put a little Charlie Chaplin animation into him as he walks down the aisle and up onto the stage."

Jennifer burst out laughing as she turned her imagination loose and got the image. Suddenly it was time to go. "We haven't warmed up," she started to say, but then laughed and said "Yes we have." For good measure I grabbed a copy of Peter Schickele's slapstick biography of P.D.Q. Bach for her to read just in case the competition was behind schedule and she was tempted to get serious again.

We managed to keep our lighthearted overview of the whole scene. By the time we walked onto the stage to perform, we felt like conspirators. It was not a conspiracy for Jennifer to win, but a conspiracy to have a good time. Our sense of detachment allowed us to explore the music with new interest and intensity, discovering drama and excitement that had almost eluded us.

As Jennifer walked down the aisle, I knew she had made a real breakthrough, and knew it even more when she left the hall to go shopping rather than stay around for the results. Jennifer's outcome was her own, and had nothing to do with judges this time. When we finally tracked her down later to tell her she had won, she was delighted and surprised, but she knew that the real winning had happened in another way.

3.
Shall
We
Dance?

While the Israeli painter, Chaim Nahor, was talking to a woman in silver eye-shadow and red boots who was gushing "simply marvelous" at a showing of his work, he caught my reaction to the paintings already on display. I was in a hurry and not in the mood for anything "simply marvelous." I had planned to take a quick look, meet Chaim, and leave. But in a breath-catching instant, I knew I could not leave until I had seen every painting. When the last guest had left, Chaim turned to me. "I think you like them?" he asked as he pulled out a portfolio that he had not shared with the other guests. I nodded, and soaked up three stunning water colors that he chose to share with me. Little by little we worked through the entire portfolio.

"Chaim, it's—I don't know how to describe this to you—it sounds crazy, but I have the sensation in my body that I have when I am dancing—when I am improvising my own movement to music."

"But of course," Chaim answered to what had seemed to me an ineffective way of expressing myself. "You see it—you feel it! That's the way I paint, and to you it comes through." His wise, wonderful face lighted the room the same way his paintings did. "In any art there must be movement or it becomes static—dead," he continued. "I paint to music, you see. Bach, Mozart, Schubert—perhaps most of all Bach. As I listen, my body feels the movement in the music just as you feel it when you dance. Only I dance on the canvas, no? I take brush and color and light, and my painting becomes a dance, and my dance becomes the painting. But of course. . . . You see it; you feel it. The instant you walk into the room I know."

Is it so unusual to respond to art this way? Why did I feel embarrassed at expressing my response to his painting in terms of movement? I had no choice, for no impressive intellectual comments came to mind.

23

I could only fumble out my inner response, and be gratified that he instantly understood. Not only did he understand; he was flattered and delighted. He had received recognition in several countries for his imaginative work. Yet my comment touched a spot in his soul that fogged up his intense eyes. Until he responded, however, I felt tongue-tied and inadequate, reprimanded by my judges.

I had quite the opposite experience a few weeks later when I attended a photographic showing. I felt perfectly at ease commenting on the perceptive eye of the photographer, his remarkable sense of composition, the imaginative quality in many of the pictures. Yet I left the show unmoved, although the subject matter he had chosen was intended to be moving, and had been dealt with in a way that showed brilliant technical knowledge.

"What do you mean," asked a friend once, "when you say something *moved* you deeply?" Good question. Hard to answer. The phrase is used too easily, and becomes fuzzy with imprecise, vague meaning.

When I left the exhibit I felt troubled, thinking perhaps it was I who lacked something rather than the pictures. I went back another day when my mood was different and tried hard to be moved. I was impressed, but I was not moved. Then I remembered the experience with Chaim Nahor, and I knew that for me the term *moved* was not imprecise, and was not a convenient substitute for more erudite terms. There was something lacking in this photographer's vision. The lighting was superb, the textures fascinating, the depth of focus carefully worked out, and the subject matter full of emotional overtones. The pictures were "correct," yet sterile. Quite literally, nothing moved. Nothing budged inside of me.

"They were not pictures to make you feel joyful," my husband said when I tried to describe my reaction. That was not the point. Being moved is not necessarily joyous. It may have nothing to do with feeling joy, although many times I do. It has to do with a strong reaction in my entire body that involves muscles and tissue and cells and emotions. It has to do with feeling intensely and totally alive and—yes—charged. The emotions that accompany the feeling may be sad or joyful or angry or tender. But the feeling of movement is there: the sense of literally being moved around at some deep level of awareness.

We speak also of being moved or not moved by music, dance, or theater. We can fall asleep at a flawless concert. Or we can go to another, feeling just as tired to begin with, and come away with an indescribable charge in our bodies and our spirits. Interestingly enough, the second concert may not have been as flawless, but the performer conveyed a quality of energy and involvement that inspired and refreshed us.

The difference is hard to pin down, and we often blame ourselves for our fatigue or flagging attention. Yet the chemistry of our bodies changes when certain people perform, and we know we could not be bored if we tried.

Chaim danced his movement onto the canvas and I felt the response in my body. The photographer *thought* his way to his pictures and I left unmoved.

Does this mean we should abandon the thinking process and slop paint around a canvas indiscriminately, or just let our emotions carry us through performing a piece without worrying about more precise details? Heavens no! But too often we rely so much on thought process that we think our bodies out of existence. Our art—or our appreciation—suffers.

I had lunch one day with Larry Graham, a performing and recording artist who had recently won several international awards and who taught at a nearby university. I had been a guest lecturer in the piano pedagogy class he was teaching, and he was skeptical about my ideas for using movement as an integral part of teaching piano. To illustrate my ideas, I described a session with Kate, a student who was playing a Mozart fantasy. The piece opens with a slow tension that I could easily demonstrate with my body, but which eludes verbal description. As the opening chords unravel, the music gives the sense of tentatively exploring a fascinating, unknown grotto.

Kate loved the piece passionately, but the passion didn't show because her head pretended it could direct fingers in such matters as passion. Those slow opening notes on the piano should sound as though they are being played on cellos or double basses or violas, where a well-rosined bow can prolong and intensify a tone, and where the body of a cello and the body of a player are almost as one body producing—almost breathing—the tone. That's a lot to ask of a precocious seventh-grader tackling music beyond her years, and a lot to ask of hammers hitting strings.

I could have inundated Kate, as I sometimes have, with a lengthy verbal description of the qualities of that opening. I could have been quite precise about the amount of weighting she needed in each finger to achieve the crescendo. I chose instead to invite her away from the piano to discover something about Mozart that heads and fingers can't teach us. We stood facing each other, the palms of my hands against hers with just enough pressure to create substance for her to work with. "Now show me with movement how that opening phrase feels to you."

Timidly, Kate started exploring. As she heard the music more clearly in her head, she let her arms flow with an intensity that matched that of the music. My own body yielded and resisted in a subtle flow of energy between us. When I felt that her sense of the music had become body-knowledge, I asked her to play the opening once again. The long notes that had seemed passive and limp now had a resonance and energy that brought the music to life.

Larry, my friendly critic, thought the anecdote interesting enough, but still maintained that the movement experience was probably super-fluous. He began describing how he feels about that opening phrase and why it works musically for him, vividly demonstrating with his hands and arms how he reacts to the dramatic tension in the music. As he spoke—with words and movement—I realized that our table had become a center of attraction in the restaurant and remarked, "Larry, look at yourself."

His arms suddenly dropped to his sides, he looked around a little embarrassed, laughed, and replied, "Case dismissed! I guess I've just proved your point."

Indeed he had, for he could never have been as eloquent with words alone. Of course, he had proved *his* point at the same time for he is a musician who intuitively feels movement in the music he plays. But there are many musicians who are so distant from their physical bodies that they need the drama of actual movement to reconnect them. Even when musicians have this wonderful intuitive sense, movement can clarify their musical responses and strengthen their interpretation. Larry was willing to experiment with this at a later point. When he did, the combination of his wonderful musicianship and technique—enhanced by additional musical freedom gained through experimenting with movement—was sheer delight. He found that moving a phrase with his body could be an interesting shortcut to sensing how to shape that phrase musically at the piano.

In my own playing, I find that although thinking verbally about a phrase gives me important information, I can always discover still more through movement. If we are tied to the verbal concept and never verify it with the wisdom of our bodies, we may fool ourselves into thinking the music sounds right because the words sound right. But words and music are not the same.

How about the listener? When we listen, does it change our perceptions if we are tuned in to movement? Sometimes we blame the performer wrongly, for at times we go to a concert and become inert lumps of flesh, challenging a performer to move us out of our sophisticated lethargy. I sometimes enhance my enjoyment by giving free rein to the intuitive side of my nature, allowing imagery to develop, characters to emerge, and invisible dancers within to respond to the choreography of the music. My muscles come to life in response, yet to an onlooker's eye I am sitting as sedately as Mr. Hacklebriar in the front row (or almost). When I listen this way I know I've hit a real loser if the music only lulls me into a state of indifference. If I play recorded music at home I need not worry about a Mr. Hacklebriar, and can turn the dancer loose whenever I wish.

All very well, you say, for someone who loves to move and dance. But is the urge to move and to dance that unusual? Or is it a natural capacity that we often ignore? Doesn't that urge to move come with our first breath of life? How about earlier, when we first stirred within our mother's womb?

As a mother, I have lovely memories of that stage when an abstract pregnancy turned into a tiny tentative quiver within my belly. I couldn't be sure at first—perhaps it was a gas bubble. Within days the tentative quality changed and I knew something marvelous was taking place. Nothing abstract any more. There was something alive in there, each day gaining power to capture my attention. Each child I bore moved differently, and I never lost my sense of awe—even though at times I wished this new little life inside me would choose a different rib to kick.

Research has shown that the fetus responds to voices, sounds, music. The newborn baby carries this response into a new world. The movements of the baby are not just random movements, but are often choreographed by surrounding sounds. By the time the baby is a toddler, no researcher is needed to convince us that the child is responding to music.

As small children, most of us listened to music with our entire bodies, charming parents and aunts and uncles with our free and joyous movement. But charming our relatives can be dangerous. Their encouragement can sow the seeds of selfconsciousness. When a natural response turns into a performance, the charm fades and we may be scolded for showing off. Alas, spontaneity and scoldings can become cousins in our minds.

At a proper age we may have been sent to "dancing class," but in all too many cases the class had as little to do with that original response to music as a rap on the knuckles at a piano lesson has to do with liking to play the piano.

That innate response is still there within us, waiting to be rediscovered. People often find themselves crying as they begin moving to music again after years of disconnection. The crying can mean many things, but frequently it means that they have been touched in some forgotten corner of their being. The crying sometimes means sadness for something they have lost and the joy/pain of rediscovery. Sometimes it signals a healthy release of emotions tucked into the too-tight bag of adulthood. People often realize how alienated they feel from their bodies, and feel nostalgia for earlier freedoms.

If sadness is experienced, it is usually a fleeting feeling, yet is important to notice because it tells us something about what we deny ourselves. What may come next is a body-tingling charge which signals that a part of us that was dulled into polite passivity before is alive and awake. In workshops I always enjoy the reaction of people who rediscover the dancing child within as their bodies come to life. Their faces change, their personalities liven up, their eyes become more expressive.

Try an experiment, just for yourself, behind closed doors where you won't be embarrassed. Get a recording of the Samuel Barber *Adagio for Strings*, the Albinoni *Adagio for Strings and Organ*, or some other record of your own choosing that moves along with a powerful sweep. Turn on the record player and lie comfortably on the floor with plenty of space around you. Imagine the music flowing into your body. Experience the essence of the music . . . let it flow up through your veins until your whole body is suffused . . . feel the sensuous quality of the music . . . let it turn you inside out . . . weep with it . . . laugh . . . let it do an inner dance of power, of ecstasy within you . . . let it flow into your arms, your fingers, your thighs, your knees, your toes.

Resist the music if you must . . . then go with it . . . flow with it . . . let it reach some inner layer until you can no longer resist the urge to move. Let the music do what it will . . . let it pull you up off the floor . . . move with it . . . play with it. Feel the air about you come alive with sound waves . . . let your body tangle with the music and mingle with the vibrations in the air. Let yourself be alive to the fingertips . . . beyond the fingertips. Feel streams of energy yield like elastic as you explore the space around and above and below you.

Feel the climax of the music . . . intensify . . . intensify . . . let it take you where it will, and leave you where it may. As the music ends, sense the life and energy in the silence. Listen for your own silence as a frame around the experience.

Or try another experiment. Take a folk dance record: an English country dance, an old-fashioned polka, an Israeli hora, or the dance music from "Zorba the Greek." At first just listen. Feel the compelling rhythm. Then begin moving, but with some restrictions: at first let only your fingers dance to the music, your feet glued to the floor, your body immobile. Let your fingers gradually connect to wrists, now to arms, and next to shoulders. Now a torso can move from the waist, feet still glued in place. When your legs and feet can stand the restraint no longer, turn them loose, but don't think about what they are doing. Don't worry about correct steps. Your body knows how to move. Trust it. Send the judgmental part of yourself off on vacation so it won't interfere, and make up your own steps.

Try it with a friend, or in a group. It doesn't matter whether you ordinarily have two left feet or not. Just pretend when you improvise that everything is right, and somehow it is. Interact with each other. Hook elbows and spin around . . . snap your fingers . . . step-hop-leap-bounce-clap . . . allow your body to respond before your mind catches up and balks. Out of breath? Your body will automatically slow your pace until you get your second wind. Surprise yourself with your gyrations? Many people do, once they drop that top layer of stuffiness. Feel more alive suddenly? A common reaction.

Some people panic at the thought of such a free, unstructured response to rhythm. They have been told—often enough to believe it—"You have absolutely *no* sense of rhythm." I don't believe it. They probably need a word of encouragement and a nudge to connect with the sense of rhythm that everyone possesses just by virtue of being alive. It would be difficult for a human being to live an *un*rhythmic life, for rhythm is inherent in too many bodily processes—the beat of the heart, breathing, peristalsis. Even though we may not be consciously aware of these rhythms, they form a backdrop or undercurrent for our consciousness, waking and sleeping. If I put on a recording with a strong beat and ask you to tap out an *unrhythmic* response, you would find it much more difficult than to respond rhythmically.

There are great differences in rhythmic abilities, however. When I have students with a ragged sense of rhythm, I ask them to show me how they crawl. It's pretty undignified, but you might try it. See if you crawl with right hand and right knee together, or whether you have a cross-crawl pattern of right hand with left knee and vice versa. People with a strong sense of rhythm usually have a strong cross-crawl pattern. People with fuzzy rhythm, on the other hand, are apt to crawl by shifting weight from the right hand and right knee to the left hand and left knee.

If you do *not* naturally use the cross-crawl pattern, have courage. You can change the "no sense of rhythm" curse if you can suffer the indignity of crawling around on all fours for a few minutes each day until you develop a strong cross-crawl pattern. Concentrate on moving the left hand with the *right* knee, and then the right hand with the *left* knee. (Those automatic cross-crawlers have no idea what you're suffering!) Be patient, for it may take more time than you realize. When it feels comfortable going forward, use the same pattern to crawl backwards, and then sideways.

If you can do the cross-crawl already but lack precision, practice until your right hand and left knee strike the floor together at precisely the same instant. You'll be pleased at how much this will sharpen your sense of rhythm. If you have trouble with the cross-crawl, and consequently with rhythm, you might be curious to find out whether you were one of those physically precocious children who walked before you spent much time crawling. According to some specialists in developmental pediatrics, skipping the crawling stage can cause a gap in physiological and neural development. These gaps are also related to the sense of rhythm.

In the meantime, forget about the accuracy of your rhythm and connect your body with music in any way that feels comfortable. See how you come to life. Not only do we *feel* more alive when responding physically to music, we actually are. Our breathing is stimulated, as is our cardiovascular system and many other complex physiological processes. We are mainly interested, however, in how our bodies actually feel, how locked up emotions can begin to release, and how we can experience the creative and imaginative parts of ourselves. It is not the same as simply engaging in exercise, valuable as that may be. We release a free, spontaneous, uninhibited being who has been hugging the wall, afraid to dance but desperately wanting to try.

Let's take things further and explore different styles of music through our newly-discovered ability to move. If you are a Baroque music fan (or even if you're not), play a recording of a Bach Suite and feel the difference in the way your body moves to a sarabande compared to a courante, a gigue, a minuet. Switch to the Classical era and compare Mozart to Haydn. Find out if you can feel in your body the difference between Mozart's elegance and Haydn's impulsiveness. Your body will pick up more distinctions than your ear. Then compare that feeling with your response to Chopin, Brahms, or another Romantic composer, and you may discover what no history book could teach you about different periods. Go on to Debussy or Ravel and discover how differently your body flows with impressionistic music. Resist the impulse to think your movement out logically.

I often encourage such exploration in a group, using movement dialogues between partners or random interactions between group members. When people allow the movement to come from inside out, without pre-planning, they usually feel a dramatic difference as they change musical eras or styles. In a group they learn not only from the wisdom of their own bodies, but from seeing and feeling the dynamics of group interaction. Using movement to explore style in this way lends fresh understanding to intellectual knowledge, and music history takes on a new dimension.

If we progress into the twentieth century and move to Bartok's *Allegro Barbaro*, the phrase "primitive rhythm" becomes more than an intellectual concept. Try moving to *Circles* by the contemporary Italian composer Luciano Berio. You will find it more difficult to dismiss this as strange contemporary music, as your body finds the flow and structure and excitement that an intellectual ear can miss.

Move to some of the pieces from *Makrokosmos*, by George Crumb, a contemporary U.S. composer, and you will never be quite the same. You may find yourself giving birth to a planet, living through some of man's tormenting and exalting emotions, and spinning off into a spiral galaxy.

Turn another corner musically and dance to classical Indian music, such as a recording by Ravi Shankar. The hypnotic drone of the tamboura in the background of the sitar and the complex rhythms of tablas will coax your feet.

I disliked rock music until I danced to it. Now one of my favorite recordings to use with groups is the classic *Inna Gadda Da Vida*, recorded by the Iron Butterfly. A friend disliked classical music until he discovered Bach through movement. Test out an acquaintance who swears she hates jazz with one of the Claude Bolling suites or with Bill Evans. Our bodies are much less opinionated than our heads.

The application to performing is obvious. A former student returned for a visit after moving away. She came for a quick shot of inspiration—to get in touch with a part of herself she felt she had left behind. Her new teacher was exciting, demanding, challenging, and I felt the girl had developed well technically. Yet when I complimented her on the Haydn style she was developing, she shrugged her shoulders and said "It's just programmed in. I don't feel it." She wanted permission and encouragement from me to dance her way to a sense of Haydn. Her comment about not really feeling the style of Haydn made a deep impression on me. I realized again how ineffective it can be to *tell* a student "Let it dance," or "The music needs to move more freely," without actually dancing or moving freely. It's like trying to describe the taste of a ripe pineapple in words.

The term "programmed in" has bothered me ever since. I had used movement in my teaching almost apologetically for a long time, for it seemed somewhat unconventional to ask someone to leave a piano bench during a lesson. Yet this student missed it. Shortly after this visit, I was asked to give a workshop at Redlands University in California, where I had the opportunity to get acquainted with Alexandra Pierce, a well-known teacher, composer, and writer. My work with movement seemed more legitimate after I experienced the genius of this inspiring woman who incorporates movement into every aspect of her work in teaching piano and music theory. Our minds danced together as we shared similar alternatives to "programming in" a formula for a particular piece. I used movement with more assurance after that.

I find the transfer from movement into performance fascinating. Something a little four-squarish begins to soften at the edges and melt away. Our intellect is supported and enhanced by our imagination. We are less apt to manipulate the drama in a tempestuous Beethoven sonata if we have felt it ahead of time in our body. The dances in a Bach suite can truly dance. We can feel, rather than think, the wildness of a Prokofief sonata. If we have physically experienced the giving and receiving quality of *tempo rubato*, our tempo changes will happen as naturally as though we were walking in a garden, quickening our steps to reach the brilliant blue of the delphiniums, slowing our pace to savor the spicy fragrance of the roses.

A university piano student came for a coaching session, ready to show me how beautifully she could play a slow movement from a Mozart sonata. She had thought the piece out carefully, analyzed it harmonically, planned lovingly for nuances, cherishing the opportunities for rubato. But her planning was too meticulous and had cowed the spirit out of the piece. I asked her to follow the music around the room, reaching for each burst of an invisible pulse.

"Keep feeling those small explosions of energy as you play," I suggested as she came back to the bench, "and don't try consciously for any of the rubato you have been putting in."

Her eybrows went up. "Can't I put in my wonderful ritard at the end?" she asked, like a child begging for goodies.

"Keep the pulse, and instead of thinking about it, just feel the quality of the ritard in your own center—your dance space inside." Her well-planned ritard had slowed too early and too much.

Her playing changed so easily that it seemed ridiculous. She was like a science-fiction character who only needed to let her thoughts rest lightly on an action and it was accomplished.

"It's spooky," she said when she finished. "I heard it—I heard a rubato. It was really subtle—and I heard a ritard at the end. It really happened, didn't it? But I didn't consciously change the speed."

The listener hears it too, and finds it more exciting without knowing why. The music *moves* the listener. But first the music must move the *mover*—must move the performer.

If you are lucky enough to have a dancing friend available, the music can also move the dancer while you play. I mean "dancer" only in the sense of someone who enjoys responding to music. I may think I have discovered all I can about Chopin, Scarlatti, or Brahms in a particular piece. Yet the instant someone starts dancing to the music I am playing, I feel it change beneath my fingers. The phrases find a more beautiful shape. I discover fresh nuances. I give myself more time for unselfconscious drama or tenderness. It is as though someone else's movement makes the drama, tenderness, or passion legitimate and more authentic. The dancer responds to my sense of the music, I respond to that person's sense of *my* sense of the music, and as we toss the energy back and forth, the music intensifies and finds a new freshness, a new magic.

"Nice theory," you say, "But I can't imagine myself trying it, not at my age." (Seventeen, did you say? Thirty-two? Forty-six?)

At the age of ninety, my still-energetic mother accompanied my husband and me to an international folk dancing class. As she sat watching the teaching for a few dances, I realized that her feet were vibrating with information.

"No, no," she protested, when I invited her to try the dance. "You know I've never danced before in my whole life." I knew.

Her eyes belied the "No, no" response, and we pulled her into the circle. Soon she was doing a two-step forward, a two-step back, in and out of the circle, as though she had danced all her life.

"I guess I've always had itchy feet," she explained through the aura of her excitement, and went whirling off with a partner who assumed she knew the next dance.

"Itchy feet" indeed! And a body meant for dancing, only it took a long time to make the discovery.

I suspect we all have "itchy feet" that need to dance and jump and spin us into new worlds. We need not wait until we are ninety!

4.
Inner
Clowns

The hour was late. The city was strange. The information on buses was inaccurate. The day's fatigue ground at every muscle in my body. At this hour of the night, though, I could at least be assured of a seat for the half-hour ride to a friend's house. But when the right bus finally pulled up, I was barely able to squeeze onto the bottom step because of a tired crowd of baseball fans returning home. I wrapped myself in endurance and hung on as the bus pulled away.

"You sardines will have to get a little friendlier," said the bus driver. The atmosphere of this grossly overcrowded bus immediately changed, and people eased open a little more space for those of us jammed against the door. The driver chatted amiably with people near him about the baseball game, cracked a few corny jokes, and even made a couple of good ones. We started in a no-pay zone, so after we left the zone passengers had to pay when they got off the bus. For passengers in the rear to batter their way through solid bodies was ridiculous. "What the heck!" said the driver. "You're all on the honor system. Get off the back and you can walk up front to pay. I trust you."

A chuckle rippled through the tired bodies as those getting off the rear of the bus hammed it up while they ran to the front with their fare. A few stolid souls resisted the driver's humor and insisted on savoring their misery. But most of the riders, young and old, seemed instantly grateful to the driver for turning a tedious ride into a bit of humorous drama. My fatigue all but vanished.

The point of the story, of course, is that delightful flip from one possibility to another that happens when someone plays clown and helps us find the humor in our shared predicament. The bus driver could have simply endured the run that evening, stoically putting up with a busload of complaining, snappish people. Instead he chose to enjoy the situation. I had the sense that he didn't think of us as a "busload" of people at all. He saw us as individuals, and as individuals we responded to his banter. I grinned at the crotchety-looking old man on the step above me, and when he grinned back he was no longer crotchety-looking. The obnoxious-looking fat kid who crowded too close to the driver was suddenly the straight man in a comedy act, and I loved him. The sour-looking lady with the black umbrella had a sudden spasm on her face that turned her wrinkles up instead of down.

Often we are not even conscious that we need a flip. I'm thinking of how addicted we musicians become to the supposed virtue of grinding practice. Yet when we practice in this way, do we really guarantee a fine performance? What we often do guarantee is tension piled on top of tension. We guarantee that muscles are punished. We guarantee a tired body, a tired mind, and too often, tired music.

When we get in this state, we need an inner clown to tickle the inside of our ribs and let us laugh a bit at our condition. We need the kind of flip that jolts us into a new level of alertness and gives us fresh insight.

Our goal is to play well. But real goals easily get obscured when one gains status through suffering. Listen in at the lunch hang-out near a conservatory some time and you will pick up this trend in a lot of conversations. (You won't even *see* the students who skipped lunch to get in an extra hour of practice.) If you wanted to do a humorous skit parodying life at a conservatory, you could lift some of these conversations verbatim for your script. "God, I worked four hours straight on the Bruch today. It just doesn't get any better. And the Bach—I don't think I'll ever get those shifts in tune consistently." "I know what you mean. I tried one shift two hundred times in a row today to clean it up, but I still can't trust it. Oh . . . my arm is so sore! Anyone have a heating pad?" "I've got one, but I need it for my shoulder. I've got an audition coming up in two weeks and if this keeps up I won't even be able to lift my violin. Got any aspirin?" "I've just got to get in at least ten or twelve hours each day over the weekend." "Did I ever have a good workout today! I cut Theory and Music History and just plowed straight on through since six o'clock this morning. Old Maestro had better be pleased at my lesson."

These are normal young people. There are thousands and thousands like them throughout the country, suffering from the same addiction. They don't call it addiction, and they don't have inner clowns who could give them some perspective. They think they are buying a future as a professional musician. Most of them first got hooked on music for the simple reason that they loved it and had some talent. But addiction it is, and it's an insidious one because it usually goes by more acceptable names such as "devotion," "commitment," and "dedication." The addiction comes from an old mystique about the nature of learning a performing art and seems to intensify with each new crop of students as the competition gets ever tougher.

I remember the times during undergraduate days in music school when a friend and I took great delight in outwitting the janitor in the music building by hiding while he locked up the building at 10:00 p.m. If we used practice rooms off an inner court, our lights and sounds were not detected from outside the building, so we could practice far into the night if we wished.

There is a saturation point for the human mind and the human body. At a certain point we do another kind of flip into theater of the absurd. "They can take it. They're young, they can bounce right back," I often hear when I voice concern over the inhuman pace music students set for themselves. Great. So they must be punished for having resilient young bodies. And when will they have the chance to "bounce right back"?

During a summer vacation I worked off and on with a violinist and a cellist from a well-known music conservatory. They were addicted to the typical heavy practice grind, as were most of their fellow students with a lot to prove and a lot at stake if they didn't prove it. By working harder and harder to decrease the tensions in their playing, they succeeded only in producing more tension that they had to work harder and harder to get rid of. They thought about practicing this way: if a passage went badly, it obviously needed more work, and if it went well, then it needed still more work as a kind of insurance policy. They probably could have seen the folly of overkill in everything but their own work. Their criterion for success at the end of a day was not what they actually accomplished during their practice, but how many hours they logged. They had no accurate way to measure their progress, so the number of hours was something concrete to produce as evidence of commitment. They were shocked when they realized that "a really good practice" actually meant eight hours of punishing work. They would stagger out of the practice room with red-hot shoulders and raw fingers, but it had been "a really good day." Those eight hours seemed tangible proof of their dedication. If they didn't make it, no one could blame them. Did *they* need some inner clowns!

Jerry, the cellist, and Diane, the violinist, sought me out because they had heard that my work with musicians was similar to Tim Gallwey's work with tennis players. A conservatory teacher had recommended that they read Gallwey's book, *The Inner Game of Tennis,* and they were interested in its practical applications to music. Many teachers are concerned about the kind of scene I have described, and are seeking ways to help combat the tension and stress. Jerry and Diane were intrigued by Gallwey's philosophy: "Trying fails; awareness cures." His approach seemed clear enough when they read about tennis players who solved problems through awareness, but when they attempted a translation into cello or violin language, their brains went fuzzy. Yet they had that interesting blend of openness and skepticism which I find healthy, and I was curious to see if I could help them discover some flips in their awareness that might lead to more effective practice.

Rather than starting with obviously difficult passages, I asked them each to play a single tone on their instruments, with a smooth crescendo from soft to loud and a decrescendo back to soft again. Although it sounds elementary, in some ways this was one of the hardest tasks I could have set for them. They looked a little disappointed, but dutifully tried. Diane, the violinist, wrinkled up her nose after her first try. I remember Jerry's sheepish grin and his "I know I can do better than that" shrug. They both had the impulse to try again immediately. After several attempts, each progressively worse, I stopped them. That was the old pattern, and we were looking for new ones.

"If you were a tennis player, how would Gallwey help you?"

"I guess he would ask us to become aware of some aspect of our serve."

"You read the book well. What do you want to focus on?"

"Maybe we should just be aware of whatever shape we actually hear in the crescendo and decrescendo," ventured Jerry. "How about drawing that shape when you finish?" I added.

It seemed a good place to start. He played again, listening intently, then drew a picture in the air with the tip of his bow. "This is the sort of shape I heard when I was trying so hard:

"But this last time, when I got really interested in listening to the shape, it began to smooth out. Hmmm. Want a turn, Diane?"

Diane was still trying too hard for it to help at first. But they continued to take turns, listening carefully, then drawing the shape of what they heard. Their crescendo-decrescendo patterns began to develop smoother shapes, more like this:

They wanted to work on tone quality next. So I suggested that they keep working with single tones and try sensing the movement through space of the hand holding the bow. This did little for Jerry. But Diane suddenly felt air change into cool substance as her hands flowed through it. With a new focus, her sound began to change.

"Gallwey asks tennis players to *ride* the tennis ball across the net. How about riding your bows into the sound?"

They went a step further and became the well-rosined hairs of their bows. The image of becoming bow hairs which could initiate vibrations on a taut string tickled their imagination, and worked well for both of them. The tones became rounder and more resonant with each experiment. It helped to ask them to tackle similar tasks, for they could hear changes more quickly in each other's tones than in their own.

We talked about what was really happening. When they changed their focus from overdetermined effort to produce a certain kind of sound, to just being interested in the shape of the sound or involved in the production of the tone in some fresh imaginative way that made use of their senses, they produced a tone in a more natural way. Checking for sensory information was quite new to them. Previously their senses had gotten into the act only by registering pain and fatigue.

"While we're about it, let's borrow another idea from Gallwey. Diane wants to work on shifting hand positions, so let's try Gallwey's bounce-hit exercise." For beginning students, Gallwey throws a ball toward them and tells them to say "bounce" when it bounces, and "hit" when they think they would hit it, so they capture the rhythm before actually trying to hit the ball. I adapted this to the violin by asking Diane to say "bounce" as she played the low note, and to say "hit" at the time the high note should be played, without actually playing it. One of the problems in shifting hand positions on a stringed instrument is to reach the high note both in time and in tune. Diane tried several times until she felt the rhythm of precisely when she wished to play the high note.

"Say 'bounce—hit' again, but this time look at the exact spot on the string where you think you should land at the end of the shift. It doesn't matter whether it is actually the right spot or not."

The first time she tried it her eyes not only went to the exact right spot, but she automatically started to play it before she remembered that she wasn't supposed to. She was surprised, because she really expected to miss it the first few times.

"Hey, I hit it—right on! I wonder if I can do it again."

She couldn't. When she consciously tried to duplicate her success, she failed.

"You know" she said, "that relates to something that has always puzzled me. When I am sight-reading a piece for the first time, my shifts are usually accurate. Then when I start to practice the piece, the shifts deteriorate. I guess when I sight-read I don't expect the shift to be accurate so I don't tense up and it just happens. That's sort of what happened right now. When I assumed it would be off, I was somehow free to do it right on the first try. The second time it felt different, almost as if I had lost my innocence! So where do we go from here?"

That's always the tough one. How do we outwit the part of our brain that wants to assume command the moment we succeed intuitively? Is this the logical, analytical "left-brain" battling for supremacy over the intuitive, imaginative "right-brain"? We chuckled as we got the image of our brain hemispheres as two different characters: the left-brain character square-shouldered and bossy, full of logical self-importance, ready to analyze and direct each action with its store of verbal intelligence; the right-brain character dreamy-eyed, intuitive and imaginative, full of wisdom but tongue-tied on the verbal side, and not very practical. We could imagine the right-brain quietly going about its business and helping to get a job done if given the chance by one of our experiments. But the left-brain character, momentarily tricked out of dominating the scene, shoulders itself right back into the act and tries to take over. Perhaps that's the point where Diane felt her curious loss of innocence. We knew this was an oversimplification of a complex process, but it gave us an image that was helpful.

"Seems like we need a little cooperation around here," said Diane. Right, for neither side can manage the job alone.

I had another idea. "Try the tricky passage from your concerto and stop immediately after the first nasty shift. Don't consciously try to keep it in tune. Just assume that for now the pitch doesn't matter. Your assignment is to listen carefully enough that you can be very specific about how sharp or flat or accurate you are and then tell us what you hear." It was like reporting where a tennis ball actually lands rather than directing it there.

It took a few tries for Diane to overcome her grimacing impulse to adjust the pitch at the end. That "after the fact" adjusting of pitch is about as effective as picking up the kids' clutter after the unexpected guest has left. When she got detached enough just to listen without berating herself, she reported "The top note is about a quarter of a tone sharp, and the lower note before the shift was slightly flat. . . . The top note was almost half a step sharp. . . ." or whatever she heard. In fewer than ten tries she reduced the size of her errors to the point of being accurately in tune several times in a row. She groaned over the hours of frustratingly unproductive practice she had spent on that passage. I asked her to describe what she had felt as she worked this way.

"Hmmm . . . let's see. Not changing the pitch of that last note was really hard. That's what I've done over and over when I practice—I knock myself out trying to get it in tune, and then when it isn't, my immediate impulse is to slide around until the pitch satisfies me. I realize that what I've been doing all this time is to practice an inaccurate shift plus all this sliding around junk at the end. No wonder I never got any better. I learned precisely what I practiced. This time, when you said the pitch didn't matter, I felt free to concentrate on things I had never felt or heard before. Toward the end I had this strange sensation that my finger knew exactly where to go, and I could finally trust it. Before, getting it right always seemed like an accident I couldn't repeat. I guess that's what frustrated me so much."

Diane was happy, but I still heard something awkward in her shift that she was missing because of her relief at having the intonation improve. I asked her to switch her awareness to her bow hand and find out how she used her bow in the shift. A cellist friend was visiting this session. I was eager to share what I was doing, although I knew he had a lifetime of traditional discipline behind him and might not approve. He couldn't keep from simmering, and finally blurted out "But you're using too much bow! Can't you see that?"

He was right, of course, but Diane was so accustomed to this kind of information that it had ceased to capture her attention. Nevertheless, I asked Diane if she could use the information my friend Carl had given her, figuring we could move on to another problem. "Sure" she said, and dutifully tried. There was little change.

I must confess I was secretly pleased, for I wanted to make the point that often we hear verbal comments and *think* we can use them, yet actually block the value those comments might have. I also knew that my approach must seem needlessly roundabout to Carl. Such a situation can seem so straightforward to someone who spots something wrong, and assumes that the other person will automatically take the information and correct the problem. We do it all the time as teachers. Although often a verbal correction *can* be all that is needed, there are times when it is not enough.

What I was working toward with Diane was for her to have a conscious awareness of how she was using her bow rather than to have her accept someone else's knowledge as she was so accustomed to doing. To help her find this awareness, I asked Diane to put her violin down and move across the floor in the same way she was using her bow. I held my breath, hoping I had hit on a helpful clue. It worked. She instantly felt that awkward whoosh of movement that was getting in her way.

"Now show us in your movement across the floor the way you would *like* to move your bow on the strings." She experimented until it felt right, then took her knowledge to the violin. The change in her playing was instantaneous. "Fantastic! Fantastic!" Carl muttered, shaking his head.

"But why couldn't I feel that before?" asked Diane. "When I moved across the floor something just clicked, and I finally understood what you were after. It's funny, Carl, because when you told me I was using too much bow I knew you were right, but I just couldn't make it change. After I moved my whole body, the transfer to the violin seemed effortless."

In the next session Jerry wanted to work with a chromatic octave passage in the Dvorak cello concerto. Octaves are hard enough to keep in tune when you move in large shifts, but are particularly devilish in this passage where you move in many small ones. He was impressed with what had happened when Diane worked on shifts the day before and thought the same principle might apply to his octaves. He played the passage, grimaces and all, and then looked up expectantly. I didn't want to respond, for I was hoping he had a firm enough grasp of what had happened with Diane to make his own applications.

He decided to try the same kind of reporting on pitches without allowing himself to adjust after the fact. Rather than start at the beginning of the passage, he played the last three octaves, dropping any demands on himself to play them in tune. We discovered an interesting phenomenon as he worked—one that I have noticed many times since. When he was sharp or flat, he never missed reporting his errors. When his intonation was accurate, however, he often forgot to report.

"Hey!" I interrupted as he got ready to try it again. "What about the pitch that time?"

"Oh, this time?" he shrugged, "It was right on."

"Then *tell* us it is right on. Say it out loud," I insisted.

"See?" said Diane, "That's what I meant when I said that if I shifted accurately I would just regard it as an accident."

Jerry grinned. "Of course. My good performances are *always* accidents."

"I guess I feel that way about a lot of stuff in my life," he added. "I sort of shrug off my successes but get preoccupied with possible failures. Pretty dumb, isn't it?"

Pretty human, we decided, and went back to octaves. His accuracy improved more quickly now that he gave himself permission to register his successes. He added more octaves one or two at a time, then took a deep breath and braved the passage from beginning to end.

"Let's work on something else," he said when he finished. "I've never played it that well and I don't want to take a chance on blowing it!"

"Okay, if you understand that if you *do* blow it next time you practice, you don't have to go back to slithering."

He chose a passage from a Beethoven sonata next. He was annoyed with the fuzziness he heard when he crossed from one string to the other with his bow. His very determination defeated him, however. I asked him to listen carefully to that wisp of sound in between.

"Listen to it? I want it to go away. I don't *want* to hear it." But he cocked an ear and listened.

"Darn. It was gone that time." He didn't understand yet that it went away simply because he allowed himself to listen for it.

The wisp of sound sneaked back to keep him company. He seemed almost relieved, for that was his *problem*. How could he solve his problem if it went away so quickly? (His clowns were hiding around the corner.)

"Watch your bow hand and see if you can *see* the fuzz this time instead of just hearing it."

Jerry caught on fast to that one, as he saw when and where and how he produced the unwanted sound. He also realized that he held back on the low note before one cross-over as though he needed to save up energy for transferring the weight of the bow to the next string. I asked him to be aware of the instant the low string started vibrating, and to feel the vibration not only in the finger pressing the string down, but to feel it in the bow itself. The tone gained resonance. "Can you feel the vibrations in your body?" I asked, for he had no concept of his body as a resonating chamber.

He was used to listening to tone; sensing vibrations was still new. His tone became rich and full, and when he crossed back and forth between strings the resonance carried cleanly from one to the other.

When we first started working, I had noticed a great deal of tension in Jerry's body. At many points I was tempted to scream *"Relax!"* as I reacted to his locked jaw and pleated forehead. I also suspected such a command would be about as effective as telling him to levitate. So I was pleased that as we worked, some of the tension released without our dealing directly with it. At this point I felt that I could help him work with the remaining tension more directly.

I let him choose a passage to play, then I asked him to pay attention to the exact amount of energy he was using in each arm, in his wrists, in his fingers. I stressed that he should only observe that energy, without judging his effort as too much or too little. Again, it was a new experience. Jerry's critical faculties were so overdeveloped that it took a while to say *"Shh!"* to them. Observation was ordinarily synonymous with judging for Jerry, and his judges usually had their thumbs aimed at the carpet. Changing was not easy—in fact it seemed impossible at first. But Jerry started feeling new sensations that interested him. "Okay, this time I'm going to close my eyes and just tune in to measuring energy." He bopped the side of his head to knock out the old pattern of measuring good or bad, and cranked up his energy-measuring meter.

"Hey, fascinating. I'm really tense ordinarily, but I just felt something let go." It seemed to be helpful to close his eyes, for he could focus more easily on measuring.

"How about measuring what's going on in your jaw?" asked Diane.

"Unbelievable!" responded Jerry after playing a phrase or two. "I ought to be able to put that energy to better use elsewhere."

"Don't worry about putting it to use," I said, for I saw that even as he sensed it, part of the tension released.

He checked knees next, and found he was clamping them viselike around the cello, diverting strength from his bow arm and from his fingers on the finger-board.

"Find out how well the floor supports your chair and how well the chair supports your body."

Jerry suddenly yielded his weight to the chair and his feet stopped resisting gravity.

He was curious about how the opening to his Haydn concerto might sound now. He wanted a strong, powerful opening, but despite some new-found releases, it still sounded forced when he played it for us.

"Put your cello down and act out the power you want." His acting was understated, as was the music.

"You're on the right track. Dramatize it now for an audience 200 feet away. More . . . more. . . . Still more! Great. . . . Keep going."

As I encouraged him, we began to see a different Jerry. The studio felt charged with energy as he discovered a convincing way to dramatize strength and power. "Go back to the cello now and see how the Haydn feels."

"Where did *that* come from?" he asked as he laid down his bow, "It felt like a laser beam pouring energy through my bow. And did you notice that my bow didn't grate that time?"

How could we not notice!

"I noticed something else," he said. "I felt larger, somehow, in relation to my cello. I don't understand it, but it felt great. Do you think I can keep that feeling?"

"Do you think you can remember what you just did to get it?"

"Of course, but it's hard to realize it's that simple."

"Power is never simple. You were ready to claim your power, or something so apparently simple would never have worked. Do you want to go still further?"

"I don't know. . . . Yeah. . . . Sure. What do you want me to do?"

"Do you remember how your body felt as you did your dance of power? Dance *with* your cello this time as you play—and carry your movement right into your playing. You may have to sacrifice some accuracy for now, but it will come back." I had realized as he played that he related to his cello as though it were an object fixed in space.

He did indeed flub the first passage or two when he exaggerated the movement. Then he felt his body melt and connect with the cello, and the movement became more subtle and natural. He gave up attacking and conquering the instrument and felt it as an extension of his own body—a much friendlier relationship. The tone gained warmth, adding to his newly-discovered power.

"You know, I have such an aversion to musicians swooping around while they play—it always looks so phony—that I've gone the other direction. This felt good—as though the music released as my body released. But did it look affected?"

We assured him that it did not. Quite the contrary, the locked position had seemed unnatural and was hard to watch. The naturalness and authenticity he had just gained in his movement pulled us into the middle of the music.

"What's funny?" Jerry asked, as Diane let out a chuckle.

"Oh, I was just thinking about what we do to ourselves in those stupid practice rooms. I got an image of the way we burrow in day after day, with someone in the next practice room doing the same—all of us feeling so damned self-righteous and hoping we can outdo everyone else in punishing ourselves." She shook her head as she pondered the image. "I can't believe it! When I think what I could get done in eight hours of *this* kind of practice! If I practiced like this, I might not have to spend eight hours, and I'd get a lot more accomplished. I might even have time for eight hours of sleep some night. Imagine what *that* would do for my playing!"

Jerry chuckled at Diane's picture of fellow students hiding out in their little cubicles, feeling virtuous, miserably indulging their addiction. His inner clowns poked another rib and turned the chuckle into a full-blown laugh. Diane picked up her violin and re-enacted the painful drama of a practice session in a wonderful grimacing parody. She locked her jaws, furrowed her forehead, and braced her knees for punishment. Our clowns held hands and our laughter brought light and clarity to our new insights.

"I'd almost forgotten what music is all about" sighed Diane as our laughter subsided. "Much as I love the violin, I've built up this thing about practicing—how I just need more time and more willpower and more discipline and more stamina and more everything. It never occurred to me that it was really more *awareness* I needed."

"You know," said Jerry, "suddenly a lot of things my cello teacher keeps telling me make sense in a whole new way. I can't wait to get back to work with him. I think he'll be as pleased as I am." Then he added, "Diane, you're right about needing more awareness. But I have a feeling that if I can just keep my sense of humor, I won't get trapped so easily. Next time you see me tied in over-conscientious knots, do me a favor and go into your act."

"It's a deal, if you promise to do the same for me."

5.
"Sure, I Had Lessons"

"Sure, I had lessons when I was a kid."

How often I hear it, frequently said with a barely-concealed groan that has to do with far more than a musical instrument that eluded mastery. It has to do with feeling dumb, clumsy, or inept. It has to do with feeling angry because your violin lesson came at the same time as baseball practice and feeling guilty because baseball was more fun. It has to do with doing what would be "good for you, and you'll be glad when you're grown that I wouldn't let you quit." Worst of all, it has to do with a love for music that lessons ignored or destroyed.

There is one story that has a strange fascination for me each time I hear it. I am always intrigued by a certain tone of voice divulging once again (though the story-teller always thinks the story is new) that the sin of playing a wrong note at the piano brought a rap across the knuckles at a lesson. It's the cue for *my* groan, which gets louder over the years. The groan is loudest when the teller is oblivious to the tragedy of the story and even takes a certain masochistic pride in it.

When I admit to being a piano teacher, I often see people's faces tighten momentarily as they recall old images of dreariness: a weekly door to guilt over scales not practiced, pieces neglected during the week in favor of learning the newest pop song, books of Hanon and Czerny accidentally lost in the bottom of the piano bench, and phony practice charts that didn't match the clock. Perhaps for some the image "piano teacher" brings a shudder of agony over the disastrous recital when your fingers ran away from your head, and your feet ran away from the platform, and your tears just ran.

Then there were the times when you could glow because your teacher said you had a "good lesson"—you were a "good boy." But deep inside, you weren't sure it was worth it, and neither were your harried parents

51

who had made sure you had a good lesson that week. The price was too high for all, even though you loved music with a passion—at least you did before you started piano lessons, and "Golly, Dad, do I *have* to keep taking lessons?" you pleaded, but Dad said he wished *his* dad had never let him quit when he wanted to and he's not about to let *you* quit, at least not until you're in junior high, and "besides, you know how your mother feels." So you decided you'd better make the most of it, and maybe Mrs. Hortendieffer would let you play something you *really* liked next week if you got through some of the horrid stuff, but the next week there she was again, hovering too close, doing her duty, urging you to "try harder," and "once again now—a one and-a two and-a one and—no, *no*, NO, can't you see that dotted quarter?" and yes, you saw it and it scared the hell out of you because you *knew* she was going to yell and you *wanted* to do it right, but your dumb brain always forgot and you weren't exactly sure what it was you were counting anyway, especially when the music said 6/8 instead of 4/4, because you had 4/4 figured out in fractions to equal one of something—one measure you guessed, but 6/8 is a fraction and so is 3/4 and it all added up to confusion. You wished you could just go home and hide and never smell Mrs. Hortendieffer's cabbage soup again, or see that bust of Beethoven scowling down at you, and why did you ever ask for piano lessons in the first place?

When you finally got home you went into the living room and pretended you were a concert pianist. You improvised wonderful sounds and there were no wrong notes and no wrong counting and you knew again that music really *was* wonderful. Just about then, Mom, who was fixing a casserole in the kitchen, yelled "Hey, stop that noise and practice your lesson."

You loved "Fuer Elise" and finally got to the point where you could play it, but the new teacher couldn't stand it because *everyone* wants to play it. He gave in, but your idea of how to play it didn't match his idea and guess who won? Little by little you realized there is one "right" way and a lot of "wrong" ways to play any piece of music, and you had jolly well better listen to whomever your current teacher happened to be.

Such images are half-humorous in retrospect, but deadly serious in reality. Perhaps you are one of the lucky ones who had the good fortune to have a teacher who supported and encouraged you, and who gave you thorough training and at the same time enhanced your love for music, for there are many such teachers. But for all too many, the words "piano teacher" set off old alarm bells.

Music lessons—or lessons in anything—can be dangerous to us, for the weekly guilt can become addictive. We can come to believe that we deserve scorn, and that we really can profit from being told repeatedly how to do it, from being given "right" answers. Gradually we lose our child-like enthusiasm for music or tennis or roller-skating or tightrope walking and substitute an intense yearning to do it "right" for the teacher. The pat on the back becomes more important than the music or the skating. One part of us becomes ever more committed to earning the pat on the back, while another subversive part—that we try to ignore—kicks and screams and resists the teacher's authority. This is the part that gives us all kinds of excuses for not practicing.

Must we forever subdue the part that kicks and screams and misbehaves? Is that part really subversive? Part of the time it clearly is. But in that rebel there is also a part to be cherished and nurtured, a part that is full of wisdom that should not be repressed. Consider the energy in this rebellious creature that could be put to good use interpreting the rebellious spirit of Beethoven. Think of that energy harnessed to developing a fine technique. What a profligate waste to expend that energy in dull tantrums of sullen rebellion! Yet how often do we get caught punishing ourselves into docility and obedience, pretending that gold stars are worth the price.

The fear, of course, is that without the docility we might not learn. What a crippling assumption! When we restrain the free intuitive spirit we cut ourselves off from an important half of our built-in learning team. We need discipline and order and logic from Mrs. Hortendieffer, but we also need her encouragement of the unruly sparks and flashes, the passions and the tenderness that convert the impersonal exactness of note symbols into living music. When we are addicted to either praise or criticism of the week's practice, we are in danger of missing that conversion process. When we get stuck with Mrs. Hortendieffer's stale cabbage soup and stale Bach and stale Mozart, it is appropriate to scream in indignation. Our fingers do not balk at being trained; it is our spirit that balks at being bullied and robbed.

We can learn to pay attention when we feel that "naughty kid" kick, and find out what it is kicking about. What passes for laziness and perverseness may be a valid reaction to unintentional bruising. I say unintentional because the teachers guilty of bruising usually have no such intent, and all of us who teach are guilty part of the time. We may get so concerned with the recital next week that we forget where it fits into a lifetime of next weeks. We get so immersed in our chosen "method" that we are oblivious to the fact that Susie's brain can't respond to our method in an intelligible way. We confuse saying numbers out loud with feeling the rhythm in our feet and fingers.

A woman named Deanne once called me with a tentative sound in her voice, saying that she had told a friend about her notion that music and movement were related and possibly could be integrated in the study of piano. The friend told her that I might be of help.

When she came to me, Deanne was almost apologetic about her strange idea, even though I assured her that I constantly work with movement to help free people musically. When I encouraged her she shared some of her background with me. She had grown up in a small town in the midwest, and had fond memories of the bubbling, dancing, joyous little girl she had been—one who delighted her parents and friends with her natural response to music. She sang and danced her way into the hearts of·anyone she was near.

Scene Two: Enter the piano teacher, who has kindly consented to give Deanne and her sister lessons. Deanne can hardly wait. Her folks have purchased a real honest-to-goodness piano, even though the ivories are chipped and snag your fingernails. A few keys stick but that's probably from the damp fall, and the pedal doesn't work but then that can be fixed. Her parents put the piano in the basement— usually a disaster, for who doesn't automatically feel banished when sent to the basement to practice? They make the necessary arrangements, and the lessons begin.

The dancing little girl soon gets the message. Piano lessons are serious stuff, not to be taken lightly. *But—I'm trying so hard—doesn't he know?* "Deanne, you must learn to count." *Just let my feet try it; let me dance it.* "Deanne, sit still. Do I have to tell you again?" *But music doesn't feel like sitting still.* "Deanne, you never have had any sense of rhythm! Now start right here on this measure—one-two-ready-start-and-ONE-TWO." *Oh no, I can't stand the sound of him tap-tap-tapping on the piano. My head can't think for the shivers in my ears.* "DEANNE, YOU MISSED THAT F♯ AGAIN." Now start all over, and PAY ATTENTION!" *I don't want to pay attention, and I'm too dumb to learn how to play the piano and I'm too dumb to learn how to count and I hate the piano and I hate him and I wish I never had to come again, ever!*

But the agony went on, because Deanne's mother was so grateful that Mr. Dirkmier would take her children. *He has such a good reputation and all the other teachers respect him, and he graduated from that music school back east, and I don't know what gets into Deanne sometimes—growing pains and sheer stubborness, I guess—but I know it will be good for her.*

Deanne never even told her mother how bad it really was, for that is the nature of childhood: we come to expect the way we are treated and often have no idea that things might be better. So Deanne's protestations were mild and sporadic, and she resigned herself to her fate and built her week around "lesson day," which had a heavy nasty scary kind of taste, and which tinged other days with that taste in varying degrees, depending upon how far away "lesson day" happened to be.

The dancing seven-year-old was gone. Deanne's joyous response to music and her confidence in her ability to conquer her world had faded into a pale memory. She felt betrayed by the very music she so loved, but she felt the hurt of being unacceptable even more deeply. She no longer seemed special and talented. Her discomfort at her weekly lesson quickly turned into shame when she was asked to perform. "I was embarrassed because I was *so* bad!" she told me. The situation was perhaps even more insidious because Mr. Dirkmier was supposed to be such a "good teacher," and because he seemed kindly enough when she just talked to him. He was a bachelor in his mid-fifties, tall and erect, with an unruly strand of lead-colored hair that would slip out of place when he was angry and fall in front of his steel-rimmed glasses. Deanne's reminiscing brought back her rage at the memory of those hard bounces of his head when he was counting out the beats, as though he could push the counting right through her own head with each thrust. She shuddered as she told me "I couldn't let the music come out, because I was in constant dread of being jumped on for playing wrong notes or for not having that damnable rhythm right."

The pieces he chose for her always seemed too hard—dreary hard, not fun hard like the ones she asked for from time to time. She was so embarrassed by his scorn for her choices that she soon stopped asking, and endured the pain of his "help" with the pieces he chose, for she knew she could never work the pieces out on her own. She memorized the rhythm whenever she could by listening carefully, and if pushed to "count it out" protected herself by a sudden streak of obstinacy, because "counting" remained an insoluble mystery. "Well, some have a gift and some don't," her teacher would sigh. Deanne decided that it must take at least forty years to learn to play the piano, and her inward sigh was far deeper than her teacher's, for there was no joy at all in this grim business.

She endured three long years of anguish, humiliation, dread, guilt and bafflement until Mr. Dirkmier moved away from the area. Deanne was without a piano teacher until junior high, when her parents found a teacher who was somewhat better. She took lessons from time to time after that, always hoping her fingers and brain could recapture that early dancing response to music. Her last experience before she came to me was one that she had while in law school. Deanne had respected and liked this last piano teacher, even though she had made it clear that Deanne was far too prone to incorporate some slight body movement into her playing. In her book that was forbidden. Ghosts from the past whispered again through one more teacher that movement and music do not mix.

In Deanne's first lesson, after she had poured out her story, we danced and drummed and improvised. The drums served as wonderful vehicles for pouring out her old rage. I discovered as she danced that the joyous seven-year-old girl was still there. I discovered also that when this girl took charge of her feet, she had no rhythmic problems. Yet back at the piano she froze in the face of a fairly simple rhythm. It was my turn to feel rage—rage at teaching that makes such a rhythmic cripple of someone with a brilliant mind and an intuitive sense of rhythm. All of Deanne's confidence in herself as a successful attorney wilted the moment she encountered written music. Even with my encouragement she still lapsed into a "poor Deanne—what a pity she has such a hard time with her music" state.

It took months of supportive work that bordered on therapy before she could examine the system of rhythmic notation in an objective fashion. Counting out loud with one's and two's was still too traumatic to attempt, but she had a breakthrough when she realized she could tap out quarter notes by slapping her knee, saying "down" each time she slapped (1), and then subdivide the beat into eighth notes by saying "down" when she slapped and "up" when her hand came up (2). She could even hold the palm of the opposite hand ten inches or so above the knee and alternate between slapping her knee and her hand, saying "down-up down-up" in a steady rhythm to match the slapping. "You mean that's all there is to it?" she marveled, and marveled even more when she realized she could add "ee" in between and after—"down-ee-up-ee" and have sixteenth notes, four in a row (3). Next she could combine an eighth note with two sixteenth notes and say "down up-ee, down up-ee, slow quick-quick, slow quick-quick " (4).

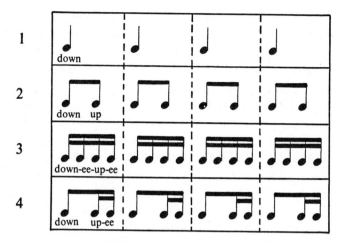

Wonder of wonders! Rhythm was no insoluble mystery after all, but a rather convenient system of symbols that could really work for her.

I wish Deanne's story were unique, but it isn't. I was married to my husband for more than a year before his sister accidentally divulged his well-kept secret that he had had two years of violin lessons when he was a child. Deanne was way ahead, for at least she knew there were such things as quarter notes and eighth notes and sixteenth notes. My husband had effectively managed to block even that bit of painful learning from his memory. He managed to laugh when he confessed his "practice habits," which consisted of propping up his music on the music stand with a Hardy Boys book in front of it, carefully placing himself at such an angle that his aunt, with whom he lived, would see only the back of the music sitting properly on the flimsy rack when she looked in the door to check on him. Then he would proceed to "saw away" while he read his book. Though he has a surprising love of music, he still has a deeply ingrained sense of the impossibility of his ever learning how to decipher musical symbols and produce music himself. I am always astonished when I meet some intelligent person who believes you must be specially endowed to be capable of learning basic musical skills.

Parents are often unwitting culprits in the drama of lessons that are intended as a gift, yet do unanticipated harm. It seems such a simple matter to send your offspring to lessons of some sort with someone who knows how to do something your child can't do. Yet it is no easy task to match up the right child with the right teacher, even with the best of intentions. The teacher parents choose may be superbly trained, but may turn out to hate kids and have not half a thimbleful of patience. And the parent may never find out. The child often doesn't confide his misgivings since he thinks it's his fault, and there is always something he can legitimately feel guilty about. He doesn't want the parents on his neck as well as the teacher.

The vague sense of guilt doesn't end with him. His parents, confronted by an indignant teacher who wonders why Johnny isn't practicing more, assume their own burden of guilt for being such lousy parents that they haven't somehow instilled that magic quality of discipline into him. The guilt goes full circle and wallops the teacher as well. If she were a good enough teacher, Johnny would obviously be *inspired* enough to practice. Double—triple binds, and often no one can quite figure out what is going on or what to do.

The guilt does no one any good, but the one who really suffers is the student, like Deanne. The focus of attention is on her, with the implication that she should *do* something: she should try harder; she should somehow be other than what she actually is. She very likely never suspects either her parents' guilt or that of the teacher; she senses only their frustration and anger with her. She would undoubtedly like to make everyone happy, but that's impossible because of the rebellious spirit that resists every effort to help her, and resists even more the helpless anger she feels.

That rebellion needs to be understood. It may mean that something is amiss with the teacher. It may mean that the parents are loading their own unfulfilled dreams onto their child. Perhaps it means that the child has some emotional blocks that hinder learning. Or it may simply indicate that the child does not fit into an accepted pattern of learning. This does not necessarily mean that the child has a "learning disability" or that the teacher has a "teaching disability." It is more an "understanding disability" in that the teacher hasn't been able to ferret out the way this particular child learns, and erroneously calls Johnny lazy. Johnny *wants* to learn, the teacher *wants* to teach him, the parents wish for success for their child, yet nothing happens. Nothing happens in terms of his learning music; yet everything happens in terms of his learning about "inadequacy."

Ways of learning are as varied as the shapes of noses. The detective work required to discover a particular child's mode of learning is relatively simple in some cases; in others it would take a Sherlock Holmes to put together the seemingly unconnected clues. It often seems much like fitting right keys into wrong locks and wrong keys into right locks, and somehow never getting them quite matched up to open the gate. The clues often hide behind vague labels such as "laziness" and "inattention" and are not easy to spot. We will take a look at some of these clues in the next chapter. Teachers and parents can spend years wandering around in circles and cul-de-sacs, thinking up ways to "motivate" Johnny without realizing that more motivation would only increase the deadlock and confusion. There may be a specific diagnosable problem in the way Johnny's brain works. Yet the child gets only the message that he is "difficult," "hard to teach," "irresponsible," perhaps "stupid." No, not perhaps—*always* that is the message: *stupid.* That message colors not only the piano lessons or dance lessons or drum lessons, but every area of his life, for a person has difficulty keeping piano lessons in one box and the rest of life in another.

Deanne was fortunate in being able to bypass her supposed "stupidity" and find a field in which she could excel. Yet although she has confidence in her abilities as a lawyer, there is always that hovering shadow of Mr. Dirkmier suggesting that the same ineptitude that showed up in his studio may show up in the middle of the next tough legal case. If the ineptitude were real, it might be easier to deal with objectively. But when the talent, the intuitive rhythmic sense, and the delight in music are all there, still yearning for expression, then going into another field never completely compensates; success in any other field still has that old backdrop of failure.

We cannot lay too heavy a burden of blame on Mr. Dirkmier. He tried very hard to teach Deanne. How exhausted and frustrated he must have been after one of her lessons. Those hard thrusts of his head as he tried to force the knowledge from his head into hers drained him as much as her. Not only were Deanne's days tinged with the flavor of "lesson day" coming up; Mr. Dirkmier also undoubtedly tasted ahead of time the discomfort of that half-hour on Wednesdays when "that exasperating little girl comes." He could bear it better when he scheduled Jonas' lesson after Deanne's. Jonas never fidgeted on the bench, never looked scared when asked to count, always practiced his scales, and sight-read so well that they could finish up a lesson sight-reading Mozart duets together. *But that Deanne! And such a bright little girl. What a shame. Just no rhythm—no rhythm at all. It's positively hopeless trying to teach her to count. I wonder if I should continue to take her parents' money week after week. And the sight-reading is no better—she just can't seem to get the hang of it. Well, some have a gift. . . .*

What he didn't realize was how great Deanne's gift was. If he had had the knowledge that we now have about the vast differences in learning styles, he could have recognized that Deanne was bursting with more music than Jonas would ever have, but that her brain perceived in a very different way. For Deanne, math and counting with arbitrary numbers had no connection with rhythm. If Mr. Dirkmier could have turned her dancing feet loose, he would have been delighted with her sense of rhythm and might have found ways to connect that sense to the symbols on the score that were meaningless to Deanne. Pointing to a note in her music and saying "This is F$\sharp$" had no connection with her spatial sense of the keyboard. If he had understood the importance of that spatial sense, he could have used it as an asset. Instead, Deanne felt deluged with arbitrary information to be memorized, but which kept slithering away when she tried to make music.

If Mr. Dirkmier could have seen Deanne in terms of perceptual differences, he would not have dismissed her gifts or lack of gifts so easily. He would have known that what works superbly for a person like Jonas will leave one like Deanne totally confused. Conversely, if he had discovered the key to teaching Deanne and had used it with Jonas, the "good student/bad student" roles might have been reversed, for Jonas might well have been baffled by the approach that could work magic for Deanne. It has taken us a long time to realize that although one mode of learning may be more common than another, there is no "right" or "wrong" mode, there are just *different* modes.

Most of us feel "learning disabled" when learning certain things. "It's not something I've ever talked about," said a friend in the field of comparative literature. "I just thought I had some unaccountable fuzziness in some areas and stopped trying to figure out why." She realized as she said it aloud for the first time how much she had suffered from this "unaccountable fuzziness." Perhaps this was why she avoided a folk-dancing class though she longed to dance—and why math was so hard! Maybe this explained why she had so much trouble learning to read music.

We are beginning to gather the knowledge we need to help people like Deanne and my literary friend. Some of them have learned music in spite of our fumbling and have gone on to become some of our most sensitive concert artists.

Others—all too many others, unfortunately—give you that funny look along with a half-embarrassed laugh, and "Sure, I had lessons. . . ."

6.
Someone Bumped the Checkerboard

Whenever I ask for directions in an unfamiliar city, I feel the same "unaccountable fuzziness" my literary friend described. I always listen carefully, yet the directions sound about as clear as a rat's maze in a psychology lab. When someone adds cheerily at the end, "Nothing to it" (or in London the inevitable "You *cahn't* miss it!"), I panic. If I start to repeat the directions, the kind lady invariably takes this as a cue to repeat what she has just said faster and louder before she waves me off with her umbrella. I barely nod my thanks, because my energy is focused on trying to keep all her information straight, and then off I start in the right direction, trying to look confident.

Turn right at the next corner . . . okay . . . go right on past the church that's across the street on your left . . . or did she mean *turn right* when I am past the church? . . . take the fifth street to your right (or was it the third?) and continue on until you come to a—oh, no, I haven't the slightest idea what I will see! . . . it could be a purple lemon tree for all I can remember. This is only the beginning, and already my brain feels like scrambled eggs.

If you have ever had a similar experience, you may be able to sympathize with Roger, an otherwise bright student, who panics if he is asked to play a moderately complex chord sequence in different keys. He starts off in great shape with everything feeling logical and straightforward when suddenly, with no warning, he feels as if someone bumped the checkerboard and the neatly stacked kings lose their heads and everything slides into a jumble. In his panic the black keys on the keyboard no longer have a discernible pattern of alternating two's and three's, but look like they've been arranged randomly by some kid. The last chord that still lingers under his fingers has no meaning whatsoever, either in the key he started in or the key he's modulating to.

Roger first came to me before his junior year in high school, already sight-reading so well that I had to gasp with envy. Yet the same brain that functioned so well in sight-reading failed him on such matters as chord progressions or trying to memorize repertoire. He resisted help for a long time. Each time I tried to help him he retreated in panic, overcome by feelings of incompetence fostered by years of clutching up over such brain-fatiguing tasks. His body reflected his fears in his square-shouldered attack on the piano, as though through such thunderous bravado he could convince himself he was really a legitimate pianist, despite his areas of troublesome fuzziness.

Roger would certainly empathize with my friend Cindy, who takes a modern dance class and finds herself listening in panic as the teacher explains a new dance sequence: "eight prances to the middle of the floor, then follow your right elbow in a circle for four steps, a lift to the left," and so on. It's new to everyone, so at first there is good-natured confusion over what goes where. As the sequence becomes clear for the rest of the class, two dark furrows appear in the middle of Cindy's forehead. I have seen her dance beautifully, but as I watch, she fumbles even the simple prances in her effort to learn the new sequence. Her body sends out uncoordinated S.O.S. messages to a brain she already knows will fail her. The darkness around her forehead increases, and as I sit in the middle of the floor with Cindy after class, her frustrated determination dissolves into defeated tears. "Everyone *else* can get it; what's the matter with me?"

I'm not sure "what's the matter," but I know that what she tells me is a re-run of recent conversations with an adult student named Ruth whose problem is the exact opposite of Roger's. While *he* can sight-read but not memorize, *she* can memorize at the drop of a hat, but shudders at even the thought of sight-reading. Cindy, the dancer, and my two students with opposite problems have all spent their lives trying to compensate for "what's the matter" with them. Whatever was the matter seemed vaguely to be some fault of their own—something to be embarrassed by and ashamed of. They'd had so many teachers who said "Now pay attention," "Quit your daydreaming," or "I know you could do it if you weren't so lazy," that they felt guilty when caught once more. When they got to those quicksand areas of learning, they told themselves "There *must* be a way to concentrate harder." Yet the harder they struggled, the more their brains rebelled and the dumber they felt. But there was also a feisty little creature inside each of them that kept jumping up and down screaming "I'm not either dumb! I *know* I'm not dumb."

Cindy had been in therapy for years seaching for long-buried emotional reasons for the inexplicable times when she felt stupid. Her therapist had helped Cindy work through every outdated trauma she could uncover, yet Cindy was still plagued with situations that left her feeling dumb and unsure of herself. IQ tests that proved her brightness did nothing to reassure her.

Ruth, my student who couldn't sight-read, had the perpetual look of a bright little kid who wants to catch on to the secrets of the adult world. She had shown obvious musical talent when she was growing up and had been sent for one summer to a famous teacher at a well-known music camp. Her piano teacher back home probably figured that a new teacher could break through some of the difficulties she had encountered in teaching Ruth. The famous teacher, however, proved herself infamous. Ruth's lessons became nightmares of humiliation. The harder she tried to force her brain to work right, the more stubborn it became in sending unintelligible messages to her fingers. Even before the famous teacher shouted at her, Ruth knew that she was massacreing the very pieces she loved, and her body would ache with shame.

The "famous teacher" was humiliated at the same time, for she knew she was failing this wistful-looking teen-ager who seemed so in love with the music until she turned those strangely reluctant fingers loose on the keys. *But she has good fingers—good hands,* the teacher would think to herself. *What gets into this girl? Maybe it's me. It must be me! I'm losing my touch. Stop, STOP! You've got it all wrong again. Why were you sent to me? Anybody else could see how it goes. You must not do this to Mozart!* And she would send the girl home in tears while *she* went back to the piano and played Mozart the way it should be played to convince herself she still had her touch, and she did indeed. *But that poor girl, what am I doing to her, she looks at me with those dark eyes that look like they're soaked in Mozart and Chopin and Bach until I let her touch the piano, and then my God, what she does!*

Interestingly enough, although both Cindy and Ruth had children with peceptual problems, for some reason they never recognized the parallel to their own problems. My clue to Ruth's problems came through her daughter, Anne, whom I had taught for some time, and whose perceptual problems had been recently diagnosed. Even so, I worked with Ruth for two months before I began to recognize what should have been apparent earlier: that Ruth herself had perceptual problems. After years of sending four daughters to various kinds of music lessons, Ruth was so eager to connect with music again herself that she could hardly wait. Yet despite her enthusiasm and conscientious practice, her old problems hadn't gone away. She stumbled through sight-reading with difficulty, and would bypass that stage as quickly as possible by memorizing whatever she was working on. But when she played a piece for me, it would be full of errors so well-learned that they were impossible to correct. She would start fresh again with a new piece, but the same thing would happen. Had I not known otherwise, I would have suspected only half-hearted interest.

One day I was working with her on interval recognition, knowing what a boon this could be to her sight-reading ability if she gained instant recognition of interval shapes on the page. I was puzzled; she was having far too much difficulty for someone who had played the piano as long as she had. On a hunch I turned the staff a quarter turn to a vertical position. The result for Ruth was *instant* recognition of intervals! "Oh, that's a sixth." "A third." "That's an octave." And so on.

I turned the staff back, hardly trusting what I was discovering.

She returned to the old hesitation; the mental counting of lines and spaces to be sure it was a fifth. Ruth was astonished. "What's going on?" she asked me. I didn't know myself what was going on, but I showed her the piece on the facing page turned sideways to keep the staff vertical instead of horizontal, and asked her if she could make sense of it.

"Interesting," Ruth said as she located groups of lines and spaces on the staff and then on the keyboard. She studied the piece more intently, noticing how the directions on the staff and the keyboard matched. Then, as she started to sight-read it, I saw the look of intensity on her face change to wonder. "This is the first time I've made sense out of this system. Why didn't I ever look at it this way before?" I was fascinated, for although I know this system works well for a beginning student, I

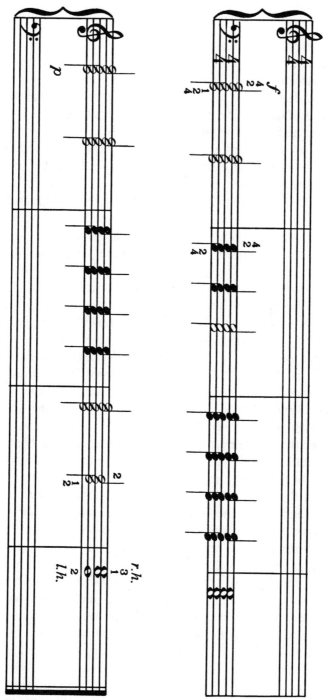

From *Bold Beginnings,* by Eloise Ristad. © 1968, 1975 The Mediaworks/Dorian Press, P.O. Box 1985, Boulder, CO 80306.

67

also know that if anyone has been reading music for even a short time, the vertical staff usually looks weird and is difficult to decipher. But Ruth's reaction was like that of someone sinking into a hot tub after a long hectic day. Finally after thirty years she understood how the lines and spaces of the musical staff formed groups that related logically to each other and to the keyboard as a whole. I write more about this sideways flip of the musical staff in the next chapter. I first discovered its significance with another adult student years earlier, and based a new approach to the keyboard on it.

We ditched the Chopin waltzes, the Schubert sonata, and the Bach for the time being, while she concentrated on the strange-looking beginning pieces in *Bold Beginnings* that were not at all strange-looking to her when she turned them sideways. I also suggested that she work not only passively as a learner, but also from the other direction as a composer. The notion intrigued her, for it had never occurred to her to try composing her own music in a system that was barely intelligible to her. She returned a week later with a satisfied glow and with several delightful short pieces written. Her sight-reading in *Bold Beginnings* had moved along splendidly, reinforced by her own composing efforts. "Ruth," I asked, "Is this the first time you ever suspected that you might have perceptual problems similar to Anne's?"

It was. Her face suddenly darkened with anger as she realized how different her lonely struggle could have been if someone had only recognized the problem. It was then that she poured out her story of all those difficult growing years: her struggle to prove she was as bright as she thought she was, the fear of being wrong one more time, the knowledge that she would have to work twice as hard as anyone else in anything she tackled, the times she had memorized ahead what some-one else could read on the spot, the hours she spent locked in her dormitory room in college trying to decipher her lecture notes, too embarrassed to go for help. She remembered the time she was asked to sight-read a new piece for the church choir when she was a teen-ager. She knew she could play the music if she had time to work on it, but the plump soprano in the back row said "Can't we get someone who can really play it?" and she fled in tears and never went back to choir.

I saw rage building that needed expression, so I gave her a Conga drum and invited her to have a dialogue with me on another drum. We drummed steadily for ten minutes or so, building to a crescendo of sound that released some of the frustration stored for so many years. When she left she took along one of the sturdiest drums from the studio, with instructions to drum daily as part of her "assignment" for the week.

The following week she told about the wonderfully angry week she had spent, waiting eagerly each morning for her husband and kids to leave for work and school so she could have the house to herself for her drumming sessions. When she had emptied out enough frustration, she explored her new concept of the keyboard and the written staff, immersing herself in both playing and composing. Her writing, charming from the beginning, reflected the music that had been locked inside for so much of her life.

I tried a lot of other ideas with Ruth, but the ones that worked best were ones sparked by the way her particular mind worked. Since she worked well with imagery, we dreamed up every possible approach that would take advantage of this. She found that she now automatically visualized the staff vertically, even though the system was so new to her. She reported that when she mentally tried to turn the staff a quarter turn around to its usual position, the lines would all squish together. I wondered how to make the staff more vivid to her so it wouldn't get mushy at any time. I suggested that she draw black lines on her keyboard for each line-note, and then mentally turn those black lines into solid tracks extending towards her from the keyboard. She could mentally stroke these tracks to get a more vivid sense of the staff superimposed upon piano keys. She imagined ping-pong balls between the tracks to represent the space notes, and little mono-rail cars running on the tracks to represent line notes. Then she got rid of the cars and ping-pong balls and imagined just the black tracks representing line notes. She took these track structures onto a white background and let them melt into heavy black lines on a page, forming an over-sized musical staff. I asked her to concentrate in her mind's eye on the black lines, then on the white spaces in between, and back to black lines. Spaces between lines began to have substance for her, and lines got blacker. "Now reduce your image to half size," I told her. "Reduce it again by half . . . and again . . . and now down to the size of the staff written as you are used to seeing it. Now blow it up again. . . . Go back to tracks on the keyboard . . . now back to black lines on paper . . . now smaller again. . . ."

When I asked her to open her eyes to a page of music, she was surprised to find the black lines looking blacker and the white spaces whiter. The black lines on the staff lost their vague quality. Notes on or between those lines grabbed her attention, and for the first time in her life sent her fingers to a definite location on the keyboard. She didn't flinch when I flipped the staff from vertical back to horizontal. We were off and running.

Whenever I tried to push some standard logical remedy for sight-reading on her, I only frustrated her as well as myself. She had already tried them all. "You just need to sight-read every day and you will automatically get better," she had heard all her life from teachers. "I sight-read every day for years and automatically got worse," she told me. It took a lot of going around the corner and sneaking up in a new direction, always honoring the way her brain worked rather than forcing it to work the way someone thought it should work.

Two other adults came to me at about the same time with similar problems, so I put the three together in a group for several months before their lives all went in different directions. The timing was fortunate, for they built a strong support group for each other. "What a relief to hear someone else describe the same kind of experience that I go through when I sight-read," said one of them.

Roger, my great sight-reader, walked in for a lesson at the end of one of these group sessions. How nice, I thought, if I could mix up the Rogers in this world with the Ruths and the others in the group, and have everyone come out with equal skill in both sight-reading and memorizing. Then again, perhaps it would be intolerably dull, and rob me of my challenges as a teacher. No, I would never want such uniformity, even though I sometimes felt as if I raised blisters on my grey matter thinking overtime about some of these vexing problems.

On an impulse I said, "Roger, tell us how you sight-read so easily. We need some clues."

"Heavens, I haven't the slightest idea how I sight-read. Let me see if I can figure out anything helpful." He picked up a volume of Beethoven sonatas and began to play an unfamiliar one.

Ruth and her co-workers, Barry and Pam, were incredulous. "You make me sick," said Barry honestly. "Is that piece really one you haven't learned before?"

"Just a minute," I said. "Roger's sight-reading is only half the picture."

"Yes, *I'm* the one hunting for help. Sight-reading comes naturally for me. But memorizing is so difficult that I tense up just thinking about it."

"How odd," said Barry. "I can't even imagine not being able to memorize. Once I get past the hurdle of learning the notes, the music is just there."

"What do you mean, it's just there?" Roger asked in disbelief. "You mean you don't even *try* to memorize?"

"Not really. Maybe I cheat, because I use my ear a lot, and I also have a feeling of the piece in my fingers." Roger wished he could cheat so well.

"How about you?" he asked Pam and Ruth. They were as vague about the "hows" of their memorizing as Roger was about the "hows" of his sight-reading. As Ruth thought about it, she decided that she had an image of the way the piece looked on the keyboard as she played it, while Pam had a more sophisticated knowledge of harmonic structure that she found helpful.

"None of this stuff makes any sense to me. I feel completely at ease in front of an audience as long as I can see the music in front of me. The few times I've tried to memorize something I have felt naked and exposed and terrified in front of people."

"Maybe you feel *too* comfortable sight-reading, and that's what keeps you from memorizing," suggested Barry. "And maybe the reason I can't sight-read is that I feel too comfortable memorizing." Barry had begun to realize that each of their strengths were enviable, but that the one-sidedness of their strengths crippled them.

Roger was indeed handicapped by the very skill that was so impressive. Since he could sight-read so easily, it was a real nuisance to go beyond the sight-reading and really *learn* a piece from the inside out, let alone memorize it. Fluent sight-reading requires a certain amount of bluffing and eyes that gulp information. It requires fingers that can simulate a fast-running passage and unwind the passage on the right beat with a flourish, an ear that refuses to shudder at notes missed, and a mind that is more intent on arriving on time than in enjoying the scenery of each measure. It needs a lot of *ham*: the ability to pretend all is well even when it is lousy going. That's all pretty heady stuff if you can pull it off. Who wants to go back to cleaning up the kitchen when you could be marching down the street in the band!

Memorizing is just an extension of cleaning up the kitchen for someone like Roger. But for the other three, memorizing felt natural and comfortable, while music on the rack in front of them was only a distraction.

Roger's disaster with chord progressions when he felt his checkerboard get bumped indicated that he was forcing in a way that would never work for him. The same was true with memorizing, for he was trying to force information into his brain in a way that defeated his natural learning preferences. He came in one day frazzled from such strong-arm attempts, but confident that he had managed to jam a piece into his brain. He was crushed when one passage seemed to stick in his memory, and he couldn't jiggle it loose. I suspected he had tried to memorize his sight-reading rather than to actually *understand* what he had sight-read.

"It went fine at home," I said before he could, and he glared at me. Then I added, "Teach those two measures to me. Assume that I'm reasonably bright, I know that there are black keys and white keys, but nothing more. Take it from there and teach me by rote, just like someone taught you 'Chopsticks' when you were six."

Roger was irritated. He had worked especially hard on those two measures, and he didn't want to play games. Yet when he tried to teach me, he quickly found some blank spots in his memory and could not tell me which fingers to put where. As I stumbled around on the keys trying to follow his directions, he had to get more and more precise in what he showed me. I chose not to be an apt pupil for him, which made him furious, but also pushed him to be more and more explicit. His efforts to get my fingers on the right keys were not wasted on his own fingers. He suddenly shoved my fumbles aside and played the passage with assurance.

"Hey, that was almost fun," he conceded. Furthermore he *had* it now. Those two measures were still there at the end of the hour and at the end of the next week.

That gave him a start on a new way to teach his fingers. I asked him to talk me through the troublesome chord progressions the same way. Again he found he had been trying to work with artificial formulas rather than from an inside-out understanding. As he understood harmonic structure better, he became more sophisticated in the way he taught a passage to me or to another student. When Roger became the most impatient with someone's honest bumbling, he became the clearest in his own head and the most eager to try it himself on the keyboard.

Interestingly enough, this same device also worked wonders for my aspiring sight-readers. Just as Roger had been reading without clear knowledge of what he was reading, they had been memorizing without knowing what they were memorizing, trusting to unexamined intuitive powers. As they talked each other through passages, they began to see patterns and structures which had eluded them before, and that made a page of music immediately more comprehensible. As with Roger, forcing themselves to read had felt dangerously uncomfortable, so they avoided it whenever possible, falling back on an intuitive skill that never took them beyond a certain point. When they explored new dimensions in the intuitive skill they already had, the opposite skill became more accessible.

Another trick that worked equally well for sight-readers or memorizers was to look at a page of music and find the spot that looked as though it would be the most difficult either to sight-read or memorize. The very act of identifying the most difficult-looking spot made that spot more recognizable in terms of patterns or harmonies or concentrations of heavy lines and notes. Often it was the sheer blackness on the page that spooked them. Once they saw what was hidden in the blackness, they relaxed.

I kept my antennae out for ideas that might be valuable for either sight-reading or memorizing. I picked up an unusual one from a visiting daughter who was learning how to juggle. "Funny thing, Mother," Rhonda said, "I practiced juggling the other day for half an hour or so, and then went to the piano to practice. I don't know whether there is any connection, but I swear my sight-reading was twice as good as usual."

You can imagine my reaction. Before the day was over I had a good start on learning how to juggle. Though I felt a noticeable difference in my sight-reading, I wasn't ready to credit the juggling yet. "Power of suggestion, probably," I thought dubiously, but went back to juggling because it was fun. The next time my threesome appeared I greeted them with my new act. Barry shook his head. "Bonkers. Really bonkers. She's supposed to be teaching us to sight-read," he said to the others.

"Oh, but I am!" I insisted, "Can't you tell?" The studio got a little wild that day with balls flying every which way. I was interested to find that after only fifteen minutes or so of working with the balls, Ruth and Barry already noticed a change. Pam, who had settled for being a poor sight-reader for the rest of her life, could see no immediate improvement in her sight-reading, but reported later that juggling improved her tennis serve dramatically!

The people who have found the juggling helpful find it hard to describe what happens. Ruth said she felt less frantic, more gathered together and present. One man, a university teacher and performing artist, marveled at how his eyes could sort out patterns more easily, especially in the complex interweaving lines of something like a Bach fugue. Another man mentioned that his peripheral vision loosened up enough to allow him to give his attention more fully to the written music.

When I myself have difficulty sight-reading, I get the feeling that my brain jams. My teacher used to give gold stars for memorizing. I got lots of gold stars, but never suspected my deficiency in sight-reading until a junior-high music teacher whom I had a crush on handed me a glee club piece to read. I can still feel the shade of my face when I tried. When I am juggling, I get into a state that is nonverbal and almost meditative. There is no way that I can use words to help me figure out which ball to catch or when to throw it. If I start thinking too hard about it, I get that familiar feeling of my brain jamming and lose a ball. When I juggle first, and then carry my juggling state of mind to the piano, I find that my brain feels somehow more synchronized, as if all the cogs are oiled and working smoothly.

I wonder if juggling would help Cindy in her dance class where she has to listen to verbal descriptions of complex patterns before she translates them into body movements. "Hold on," she could tell her dance teacher. "Give me four or five minutes to juggle first before you describe the next sequence." Or when the lady starts waving her umbrella at me to tell me how to find Trafalgar Square in London, perhaps I could pull out my juggling balls and straighten my brains out ahead of time!

It never occurred to me to wonder if juggling would help Roger with his memorizing, but he came in one day asking if we could work with the balls before we started working on memorizing. An earlier attempt at juggling had been a disaster, and it was clear that Roger was not cut out for a juggling act on our downtown mall.

"I don't mean juggling," he said, when I did a double-take. "I just want to work with throwing the balls." His difficulty with even this elementary skill indicated one more puzzling piece in the puzzle that was Roger.

We began simply by throwing and catching one ball, then added a second. I threw my right-hand ball to his right, then my left to his left, setting up a cross pattern visually. We tried an "inner game" trick when he got tense about catching. "Stop worrying about whether you catch it or not, and just pay attention to the lettering on the ball as it comes towards you." When he saw the lettering, he really saw the ball, and was more apt to catch it. It also helped when he watched the shape of the arc the ball made in the air, or listened to the sound as it plopped into his hand. His catching got smoother and more sure.

At one point Roger took off his glasses and said "I want to try something." His vision without glasses was about half his normal vision, yet he still caught the balls. "Let me try something else. I'm going to close my eyes when the ball gets to the top of the arc and see what happens." Interesting experiment, but I didn't think it could work. But Roger caught the ball on his second try, and on his third and fourth.

"Hey, let me try that," I said. He threw; I cheated. It was surprisingly hard to make my eyes turn loose of that ball. We tried several more times before I could get my eyes to close. Plop! Like magic, I felt a ball materialize in my hand. "I don't know what all this has to do with memorizing Mozart," I said, "but it's pretty astounding." I always enjoy the look of disbelief on someone's face when I try this experiment on them. No one ever expects it to work, because they always half suspect that someone else is cheating and not *really* closing his eyes.

"What prompted you to work with juggling balls today?" I asked Roger.

"I was just curious. You keep talking about how it helps people with sight-reading. I wondered if it might have any effect on memorizing." Since actual juggling had proved impossible, he had wanted to practice first only with throwing. Since the throwing and catching had gone to an interesting level, I wondered if there might be any noticeable effect.

Back to the piano. Back to Mozart.

"Hey, I don't know whether I'm imagining it or not, but this is the easiest time I've ever had trying to memorize anything," he said after fifteen minutes or so of intensive work.

He wasn't imagining anything. We found that each time he clutched up about memorizing after that, he could loosen things up by working with the balls. It always seemed to clear his head and get his brain fine-tuned for the job, just as it does with many sight-readers.

We discovered an important, unexpected bonus: a work-out with the balls not only gives the brain a boost, it also gives hands and fingers an unbelievably good warm-up. It's great for pianists, string players, clarinetists—anyone who needs strong agile fingers on his instrument. Lacrosse balls, standard for jugglers, are the best to use, though tennis balls will do for a start.

My theory on all this? I believe the juggling or even the throwing and catching with alternate hands stimulates some complex interaction between the two brain hemispheres. Certainly juggling involves eye-hand coordination and timing similar to that in playing music. Whatever it is that happens, it seems worth remembering and experimenting with further. A woman who had worked conscientiously on memorizing a Brahms rhapsody found that whenever she got to a certain measure she would blow it. We worked from every possible angle on awareness, yet she still blew it. What finally worked? A fifteen-minute session with juggling. Somehow her brain connected with her body and there it was—the whole passage—finally comfortable and playable. The jangles left her body and she was free to make use of her previous work. It's a pretty neat trick to keep up your sleeve.

At the end of several months' work together, the three memorizers, Ruth, Barry, and Pam, realized that sight-reading would never be as easy for them as memorizing. However, Ruth came in one morning saying "I'm ready to get back to work on repertoire and keep the sight-reading going on the side for fun." For *fun*? That sounded like progress! All three felt they could now be grateful for their memorizing talent rather than feel guilty about using it as a crutch to cover up their poor sight-reading. They could accept that minds rarely work equally well in all directions: we each have strengths and weaknesses. The deficiencies are not willful lapses on our part designed to annoy teachers and superiors, but are often brought about *because* of our strengths. A strong tendency to memorize may crowd out the sight-reading in the early stages of learning piano. If the reading becomes scary, and we throw in a good dose of guilt, we're in trouble. Switch the story around for the natural sight-reader. A few teachers along the way boost our guilt, and we have a lifetime game going.

Recent research on brain functioning is shining a flashlight into some of these dim corners. We are discovering that no two brains work alike. Since we can push a lot of brains into working in a fairly logical, verbal way, it's tempting to assume that this is *the* way brains work. When we run across brains that work splendidly in a different, more intuitive, more nonverbal way, making rich use of imagery and spatial relationships, we point only to the lack of the recognized mode of working and say "Aha, perceptual problems. . . ."

Remember when I asked Ruth "Have you ever suspected you might have perceptual problems like your daughter?" in a very teacherly way. That would have been no great help to her if we had dismissed the problem once we had a convenient label. I am glad that we had the courage to go beyond the label to some illuminating experimentation. I feel pretty humble when I think of the students whom I have failed over the years because I didn't get even far enough to realize that they were battling such problems. I just lay awake nights stewing about the bright musical kid whom I couldn't teach to sight-read. The bright musical kid lay awake nights smarting over being so dumb.

The same child caught in our school system can end up feeling dumb so often that he starts using his easily available imagination to think up mischief to cover up his failings. It's an easy oversimplification, yet how many delinquents are basically bright, sensitive kids whose learning pattern is so individual that ordinary teaching tactics don't make a dent? I have a friend who graduated at the top of his high school class of 800 students, went to a top university with a full scholarship, and on to a brilliant career. Yet his second grade teacher had complained to his mother that he was the class nuisance and showed such severe learning disabilities that he was undoubtedly retarded. He could barely read until he got to fifth or sixth grade, and his memories of music classes are sheer pain. The scarring is deep, for many years of his life ground by before a high school teacher spotted the fine intelligence behind the prankster, and encouraged him to put his energies to better use.

How many such students get lost and are never rescued? Yet we keep pretending that there is a correct model of a working brain and that it is our duty to refashion each brain to fit the model. Many of us still feel guilty when someone bumps our checkerboard. It's time to realize we don't need to feel guilty; the people who bump our checkerboard just don't realize we're not playing chess!

7.
Journey With a View

While hiking in the mountains once I was impressed by the fact that most hikers keep their eyes fastened on the trail immediately in front of them. When hikers meet they usually give a brief greeting as they glance up. Then their eyes lock back into place again a few feet ahead.

I decided to experiment with a different kind of looking. My husband and I were on a typical hiking trail in the Rocky Mountains, the stretch ahead generally uphill, with rocks jutting up at random in the trail. I was curious about how many times I actually needed to look down in the next thirty or forty feet, and decided that my priority would be to see and sense as much as I could around me. So, letting my feet risk a little, I let my eyes drink in the scene around me. I found I had missed much of the beauty surrounding me, and knew from watching other hikers that they were missing as much. As I allowed a soft easy taking-in of the trail ahead, I found I seldom needed to lower my eyes to the spot just ahead of my feet. That spot became part of an overall awareness of my surroundings, and I found, to my surprise, that my feet usually knew precisely where to go, how to adjust to the tilt of a rock I might step on, or how to carry me around a larger rock. I had a curious sense of detachment from my feet, and at the same time a sense that they were more connected to my body than when I guided each movement with my eyes. There was a feeling of softness and resilience in my body that I liked—a feeling of trust.

When I went back to the eyes-down mode, I felt parts of my body go "on hold." It seemed paradoxical that when I assigned the role of over-conscientious guide to my eyes, I created tension and rigidity. On the other hand, when I indulged my eyes, my other senses came to life also, bringing a sense of ease to my whole body. Occasionally my eyes knew instinctively that they needed to double-check an obstacle, and did so in a split second. Then they went back to the visual pleasures of cumulus clouds nudging mountain peaks or the brilliant flash of a mountain bluebird.

I asked my husband to follow me and see if he could detect any difference in my walking. He immediately sensed the freer stride when I was not watching my feet. This surprised him, because he first thought the experiment a little ridiculous. As I continued, I found the experience quite exhilarating and at the same time almost meditative. I could feel my body flowing through the mountain air, each whoof of breeze a new delight. My ears were free to tune in to the audacity of jays and chickadees and ground squirrels, or to the music of wind-stirred aspen leaves. The more I sensed my entire body, the more effortless the climb became and the more nourished my muscles felt from the activity. Instead of shoulders scrunching around my locked visual field, my chest lifted with each breath.

How strange to realize that something so natural had come as a revelation. It was obvious from observing the people we met that I was not alone in my lack of insight. Only when they stopped to catch their breath was it permissible for most hikers to enjoy the scenery and the sunshine and the tingle in the air. Then back they went into over-directing their feet, step-by-step, monotonously wending their way to some chosen destination above: perhaps a mountain lake, the top of a pass, a waterfall, or a mountain peak. I realized how dangerous a *destination* can be. If we put our energies only into getting to our destination or reaching our goal, we block our sensibilities along the way. We pretend that arriving is of utmost importance, and put our mind to work overtime in seeing that we get there. Once there, alas, the habits of the journey remain, and we soon spoil our enjoyment with plotting the next stretch or the return trip.

We often give our minds a too-exclusive role in the mind/body relationship. Our senses play ever less responsible roles, like children who become convinced that mother really does know best and thus lose their capacity for growth. In giving the mind a too-powerful role we cripple it as well as the body, just as a mother who "always knows best" cripples herself as well as her children. When I fall into this temptation to share the obvious maturity of my wisdom with my own children, I always lose. I miss the freshness of their perceptions which can become the new leaven in my own. When my mind gets overly bossy, I miss the perception of my senses.

In this new way of hiking I can glance briefly at the trail some distance ahead, then trust my body to absorb information without constant interference or manipulation. It's remarkable how my peripheral vision works without my being consciously aware of it. It meshes automatically with that first brief glance at the trail ahead, and translates into foot-knowledge if I allow it to happen. However, if I consciously try to focus on that peripheral vision, it becomes a strain and spoils the flow.

How often in life do we do the same kind of eyes-down plodding with an over-abundance of directional information from our minds: *careful, now, to say the right things in that job interview . . . don't make those exciting plans unless you're sure you can follow through . . . better be cautious about this new friendship . . . finish this job before you plan your trip . . . careful, careful, watch your step, don't stumble, keep your eyes on the trail.* We accept this tyranny because it is so familiar. Authority figures all along the way have trained us all too well. Small wonder that our minds take over the authority role in constantly dictating to our bodies. In hiking I found that if I glued my eyes to the close-up view and tethered my body to my instructions, I often misjudged the angle at which my foot should contact a rock. In fact, a number of times I gave an uncomfortable twist to my ankle this way. But when I looked twenty feet ahead and was aware of the view surrounding me, I was constantly surprised at how magnificently my feet worked. Without interference, they usually sensed the precise angle that let my body swing on by effortlessly.

When we *over*-look, *over*-try, *over*-instruct in our lives, we do the same ankle-twisting stumbling. We miss the essence of an experience as a constant discovery, a consciousness of being, a journey with a view of peaks and far horizons rather than a necessary trudge along a dusty pathway. When we wake up our awareness, we become like a mustang galloping above a canyon rather than a workhorse stumbling along with blinders, guided by the presumed expertise of the mind-master. This does not mean that we can abandon the mental processes so necessary in learning. It is more that we create a mutually supportive team, a partnership of mind and body. Without assigning overblown value to one or the other, we eliminate tyranny from either. In so doing we come to a new appreciation of the vast potential of our minds and bodies for working conjointly, each enhancing and supporting the function of the other. Information from our minds can be translated instantly into activity of the body, it can also be stored, and the mind does not need to discriminate between what needs to be retained or rejected, for the body does that automatically if given the chance.

I was reminded of my new insights about hiking the next time I worked with a student on sight-reading. When reading piano music we actually have two trails to deal with simultaneously—one trail on the printed page of music and another over the terrain of the keyboard. Our attention to the printed music is crucial. We are in trouble if we can't trust our fingers to wend their way accurately through twisting trails on the terrain of the keyboard without constantly glancing down at them and disrupting the flow.

In teaching a blind student a number of years ago, I was impressed by the ability of his fingers to "see" a keyboard, just as feet can "see" a trail. Since Mike had perfect pitch, he cheated at first by pressing down a key softly enough to hear the almost inaudible pitch; then he adusted his fingers accordingly. I had to insist that he "look" at the keyboard carefully with his fingers, and become familiar enough with the terrain that he could hike his keyboard trails with assurance. He became so adept at this that I became curious about sighted students. Sure enough, when they experimented, they discovered they could also find their way around the keyboard with "finger-sight." When they opened their eyes they appreciated how easy it was to keep their eyes on their music without constantly checking up on fingers, and found they could still see what their hands were doing by using their peripheral vision. Before they experimented, they were almost totally oblivious to their peripheral vision; now they realized what an asset it was.

To reinforce this sense of peripheral vision, we experimented with walking up the front sidewalk and up three steps onto the front porch of our turn-of-the-century brick home where I have my studio. I allowed them one glance at the steps before they started walking, then asked them to keep their eyes aimed generally towards the front door, at the same time keeping a soft visual awareness of the shrubbery and surroundings. They were to walk towards the steps with full stride and see if they could go right on up without hesitating or looking down. I have used this exercise many times since. Some people surprise themselves the first time they try it; others need trial after trial before they begin to trust their downward peripheral vision to guide their feet.

When students go back to the piano after doing this, they are far more conscious of their visual range. When they actually need direct visual contact with the keyboard, it is available. I have always been suspicious of the "eyes straight ahead and *never* look down at the piano" school of thought. That seems as foolish as making the hiking experience into some hard and fast rule that says "Never ever look at your feet," even when your common sense or curiosity yells "Look!"

The superb sight-reader can glance at the trail ahead in the music, taking in melodic patterns, chord shapes, big obstacles and small, and wend his way through without focusing on each note on the page—looking down only when it is crucial, and moving along freely without a break in continuity. This is not easy to do if we have been locked into note-by-note accuracy. We have to sacrifice something we may have clutched at for a lifetime: the ingrained sense of having to *make* ourselves do it right, of keeping our eyes glued to each step we take. We need to be able to trust our peripheral vision, our grasp of shapes and patterns, the tactile sense of our fingers on the keyboard—our feet on the trail. We need the courage to step blithely over or around some of the obstacles in order to reach our destination on time.

One woman, bound by the perfectionist's need to play each note on the page, was terrified of sight-reading. I wanted to shake her loose a bit from this crippling affliction, so I handed her the score of a Pierre Boulez sonata. I figured that the sheer impossibility of accurately reading such music might at least joggle her funny bone.

She didn't think I could be serious in asking her to read such a difficult contemporary score. She saw only a jumble of notes defining musical gestures that hop-scotched wildly over the entire keyboard with no familiar patterns. I assured her that I wanted only a *fake* reading of the score. She had heard David Burge, well-known performer of contemporary music, perform the piece, so I suggested that she act the part of David performing. "No hesitations, no stumbling, no looking at your hands and trying for right notes. Convince us that you really know what you are doing. Just use the score for a general diagram of gestures and dynamics, and go to it."

Being an actress as well as a musician, she was interested in the challenge and began to see a graphic shape in the placement of the notes. She certainly did not play the sonata as it was written. Yet she gave a convincing performance. Somehow she captured a sound that, surprisingly, captured something of the essence of Boulez' music. There were dramatic bursts of sound contrasting with delicate stirrings, punctuated by pauses and bunched-up masses of sound. She had a *long view* of the piece, and conveyed that view to us. She was indeed only acting, yet she had a score in front of her—with peaks and valleys and flocks of birds and puffs of clouds—that elicited Boulez-like responses in her fingers. Those were the same fingers that were ordinar-

84

ily too frightened to read easier, more traditional music.

I find that much contemporary music yields its flavor quite readily when treated this way. People are often astonished when they listen to a professional recording of the music after they have done a fake reading, for they find they have made important discoveries about the nature of the piece. They may think they hate contemporary music, yet once they fake it they often discover something intriguing they hadn't suspected. If they are curious enough, they may get tempted into actually learning the piece. A number of my students have succumbed to this temptation after doing fake readings of some of the marvelous graphics in George Crumb scores, such as the following:*

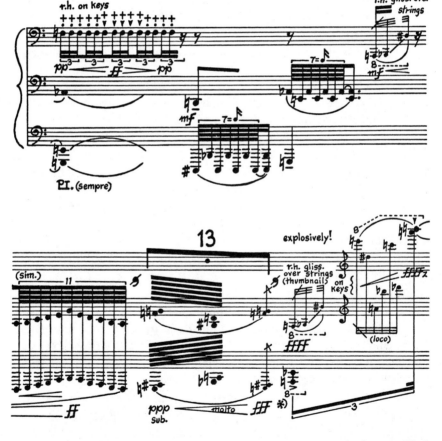

*From *Makrokosmos,* Vol. I, Twelve Fantasy Pieces after the Zodiac for Amplified Piano, by George Crumb. Two excerpts from No. 1, Primeval Sounds (Genesis I) [Cancer] pp. 6 & 7. © 1974 C. F. Peters Corporation, 373 Park Ave. S., New York, NY 10016. Reprinted by permission.

We went that day from Boulez back to Bach, interrupted by a walk up the front steps until everyone in the group had a sense of the long view. We went back to patterns and shapes and discovered how our fingers can sense the infinite variety in keyboard patterns, just as feet can sense the infinite variety in the shapes of rocks. As in hiking, our eyes take in more information at a glance than we might suspect.

I often show pianists having difficulty with sight-reading a group of five or six notes for just an instant and ask them to play what they *think* they saw in that flash. I always give them permission to be wrong. Otherwise they are apt to try so hard that they clutch and consequently fail. I also give them permission to start on any note they wish and try only for the correct *pattern* rather than the right notes.

People are apprehensive at first, since I give them no time to ponder, and they usually miss the first few tries. They quickly gain confidence, however, as they find how often their instant vision gives them the correct pattern. Though I stress clearly that I don't want them to consciously try for the right beginning note, their fingers often find the right note automatically. Yet these are the same people who keep struggling to find notes when they sight-read. If I give them more time to see each pattern, they get fumbly again, for their eyes lock on each individual note rather than the *pattern*. It's like stumbling over the very rocks you try to avoid in the trail, rather than trusting your instant vision to give you the pattern of the trail that guides you without further interference.

When people read patterns in this new way, they are surprised to realize that the complexities of reading music sift down to three possibilities in a melodic pattern: tones can move up, move down, or repeat—not many choices, when you think about it. We can elaborate on that by asking how far up or down. There, too, we can expand by realizing that the movement up or down can be one of three types:

1) We can move to the next white key in either direction (a to b to c . . .). Each white key has a letter name, and is represented by a line or a space on the musical staff.

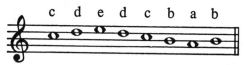

86

2) We can use the black keys to take little half-steps between the white keys with letter names. A note a half-step higher is called a "sharp" (♯), and a note a half-step lower is called a "flat" (♭).

c c♯ d d♯ e   b b♭ a a♭ g g♭

3) We can move more than a step at a time, leaving out some of the lines and spaces between.

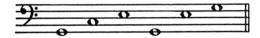

Recognizing the space between notes, called an "interval" is important, and is quickly learned if we trust our instant visual sense. An interval of a third (count 1-2-3 as you go from one line, to the space next to it, to the next line: line-space-line) looks different from a fifth, which looks different from a seventh, though they all use two line-notes.

Third   Fifth   Seventh

The same intervals can also be written using space notes instead of line notes:

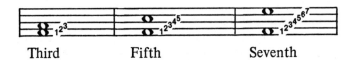

Third   Fifth   Seventh

Likewise an interval of a second looks different from a fourth, from a sixth, and from an eighth (or octave), though they each use one line note and one space note. Try them on the piano and sense how different they feel under your hand.

Second   Fourth   Sixth   Octave

The same process, using instant vision, works in reading chords—several notes played at the same time. Your eye can tell you the difference between chords in one quick glance. You need not waste time in reading each separate note. If you recognize the bottom note plus the *shape* of the chord—in other words the intervals between the notes—you have all the information you need. It's a much quicker reading process than reading each individual note. Though we usually read chords from the bottom up, it doesn't really matter. If your eye grasps the top note in a particular chord, or the middle note, you can orient yourself to the rest of the chord from there.

Take a look at the following chords and you will see what I mean about instantly recognizable shapes. For the non-pianist I show the corresponding shapes on the keyboard so you can try the chords out under your own fingers and not just take my word for the difference in feel. The numbers are for the fingers of the right hand: 1 for thumb, 2 for index finger, etc. Orient yourself to the piano keyboard by the alternating groups of two and three black keys. The area shown is from the center of the keyboard. Play the chords with the right hand. Use the fingering suggested, or try out your own if you wish.

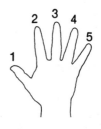

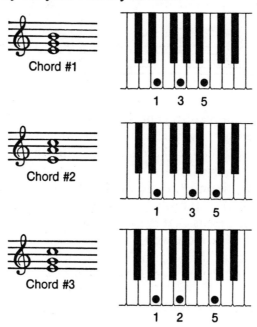

Chord #1

1   3   5

Chord #2

1   3   5

Chord #3

1   2   5

88

Now try something. Play chord #3 again. Really sense its shape under your fingers. Keep your fingers in the position of the chord and lift them off the keyboard. Do you still see the shape of the chord in your fingers? Do you still feel it? Put your fingers back on the keys and see if you can retain the right spacing between your fingers. Now keeping the same spacings, move your whole chord to the next white key to your right. All three notes will shift one note to the right. Go back to the left again. You can play that shape anywhere on the keyboard. Likewise, I can write that chord in different places on the musical staff and it will still have the same shape. It can be written either line-line-space or space-space-line, still using an interval of a third for the bottom two notes of the chord and an interval of a fourth for the top two notes.

Take a very quick glance at the following example of music, from Dmitri Kabalevsky's *Toccatina,** then cover it up and go on to the next paragraph.

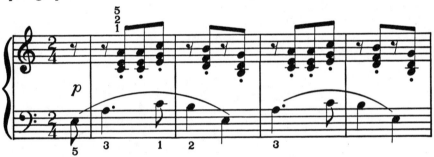

If you are a non-pianist, your first reaction was probably the usual one of considering the written music incomprehensible. Now uncover it and go back. Check the chord shapes on the upper five-line staff.

You can recognize a familiar chord shape used over and over. If you tried out any of this on a keyboard and played around with it a bit (or if you are a pianist), you probably also got an instant reaction in the muscles of your fingers as they recognized a shape.

Play around some more with this chord shape on your own, always keeping the size of the gaps the same as before. . . . Now play any single low note on the left side of the keyboard with your left hand and repeat it from time to time. You are going to move your right hand around, but *not* your left hand. With your right hand find the chord shape you have been working with, anywhere on the piano. Move around with the chord, perhaps going one note to the right, then move back to the left, or repeat the last chord, or whatever, *always keeping that same chord shape.* For simplicity, stay on the white keys. At times the sounds will seem settled and secure while at other times they will feel restless. Listen to the dissonance of those restless sounds and enjoy the calm when you hear a sound of resolution. Remember that you need not ever have touched a piano for this to work. You are just combining the simple formula of a basic chord shape with the intuition of your own ears. Now try a different note for that repeated sound in the left hand until you find what satisfies you most. The low note you choose will determine what is called the "major" or "minor" or "modal" quality of your improvisation, and will evoke different moods. Let me emphasize again: don't back off from any of the chord sounds—just move on through with a little fake assurance, pretending that you intend every sound you play. (Pretty amazing! You didn't realize you had such talent!)

Now look at Kabalevsky's *Toccatina* again. Do you feel an impulse in your fingers when you look at that chord shape? You have developed a kinesthetic feel for that chord in your fingers from having improvised with it. You can do the same with other chords.

I am amazed at how many pianists who took piano lessons for years while growing up, still have only wispy notions of what sight-reading music is all about. They are still trying to "remember where all the notes are," but have no grasp of relationships such as those you have just explored. This lack became dramatically apparent when I once undertook teaching an adult friend. Ginny had suffered through a traumatic childhood experience when she accompanied her older sister to a piano lesson. As her sister put on her snowsuit and boots after the lesson, five-year-old Ginny wandered over to the piano and played one of her sister's pieces by ear. The joy of her discovery was quickly turned into a sense of shame when her sister told on her at home. Ginny's mother punished her severely for her unwitting transgression. "When you are old enough, you can learn to play the piano the *right* way. But until then, you stay away when Kate is practicing or taking a lesson—understand?"

Ginny did not understand, for how could something so lovely be bad? When it came time for her to learn the "right way," the right way seemed like even more punishment, for it made no sense. The way Ginny organized information in her young brain differed so much from the way the method book and piano teacher organized it that the whole process had no connection with the music that Ginny loved so passionately. With the constant threat of punishment if she explored the piano in her own satisfying way through the intuition of her ears, she was caught in heart-rending frustration. When she tried desperately hard to remember *all those notes,* the notes had a way of slithering around in her mind at such a pace that by the time she forced them to stand still for her, the music was gone and she had only a dreary succession of frozen notes.

I knew part of this story in advance, and was pleased with the challenge of teaching Ginny. I could hardly wait to bring "the light" to my friend, whom I knew was brilliant and perceptive. But as we sat down to the first session, I became less and less sure of either my teaching ability or of her brilliance. I had a disturbing amount of trouble answering her questions about reading piano music, and was so shaken that evening that I took a book of manuscript paper and a pencil and sat down to figure out what the mystery was all about.

I don't know how long I sat looking at the bare lines of a musical staff, with a treble clef 𝄞 imposed on one set of five lines, and a bass clef 𝄢 imposed on the other set. There was some piece of this whole puzzle that was missing for Ginny, and I had no idea how to find that missing puzzle piece.

At some point, however, I turned the page of manuscript paper sideways, and had a sudden flash of understanding. With the lines vertical on the page, they suddenly connected with the piano keyboard!

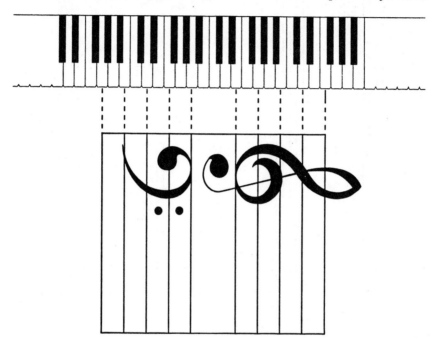

Ginny had asked perplexing questions about up and down and sideways, questions that seemed irrelevant to me at the time. Now they seemed wonderfully relevant and sensible. With the lines vertical instead of horizontal, right and left on the staff matched right and left on the keyboard. My pencil moved swiftly as I composed a piece of music sideways—a piece using all the line-notes of the staff and moving from the lines to the four space-notes between the lines. As I began experimenting, those lines and spaces began to speak to me in new ways.

The piece (illustrated at the end of this chapter) that wrote itself that night coaxed me into writing more. Eventually I expanded the concept into *Bold Beginnings,* a piano method that initially startles most teachers, for the student is asked to play five notes at once at a beginning lesson, with the suggestion that the music be turned sideways as shown on the following page. But the method does not startle the student, because the inner logic of the system meshes with simple relationships. Even a seven-year-old can play five notes at once (using

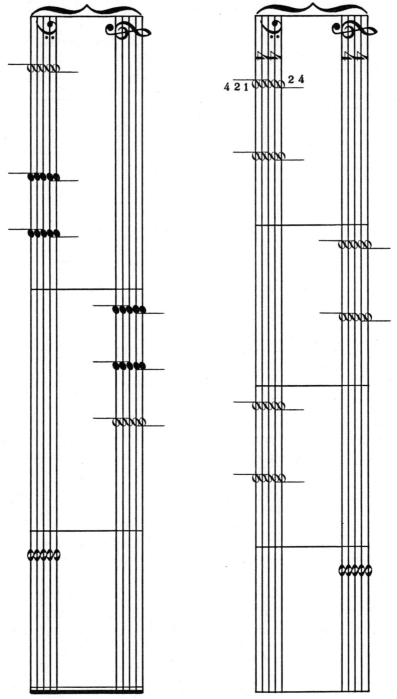

From *Bold Beginnings,* by Eloise Ristad. © 1968, 1975 The Mediaworks/Dorian Press, P.O. Box 1985, Boulder, CO 80306.

92

two hands), and can do it with great gusto. It's like giving a child, or an adult, a good-sized rock to climb over rather than a lot of small rocks that keep shifting and sliding under his feet. The latter is often what happens when someone is asked to learn dozens of notes one by one.

The experience was, again, like walking the trail with a long view and not watching my feet. It was a perceptual flip, triggered by what seemed like ridiculous questions. I had to refuse, for the moment, to accept that the usual, traditional way of teaching piano was the right way or the only way. I was frustrated enough to become terribly curious about something I had never before thought to question. Instead of turning a soprano on her head, I upended a centuries-old musical staff and found unsuspected logic.

The result was a book that speaks to the many children and adults whose perceptual mode does not match that of the authors of traditional method books. These people, like Ginny, breathe a sigh of relief when they grasp a logical relationship between the musical score and the keyboard.

Look again at the beginning piece from *Bold Beginnings*. If you are a pianist, you will find this to be strange-looking music. Stop tilting your head, though, and recapture your innocence as you look at the musical staff written vertically. Pretend you have never seen piano music before, and that you are terribly curious about this system of over-sized dots and lines and symbols that enables certain privileged people to "make music." As you look at the music written in this direction, squint just a bit and throw your eyes a little out of focus. This helps you to perceive it differently.

Close your eyes and mentally enlarge the staff until each line on the staff connects with its proper place on the keyboard. Play around with that image a bit. Mentally write some notes on this over-sized staff. The directions on the staff now match those on the keyboard. Right is right and left is left.

Ordinarily, *up* on the musical staff is to the right on the keyboard, and *down* on the staff is to the left on the keyboard. It was this "up is right and down is left" twist in reading music that left Ginny's mental shoelaces untied and dangling. The connection of lines and spaces to the keyboard had seemed totally arbitrary, devised to punish little girls caught in the act of playing by ear.

When I showed Ginny the piece I had written vertically, I watched thirty years of frustration and supposed stupidity in musical matters begin to melt around the edges. It was almost hard for her to accept the persuasive logic of the new way, for she was so accustomed to the burden of her failure to understand. It was fascinating to me that the music did *not* look as though it were written the wrong direction to Ginny. Indeed, this was the first music she had seen that looked *right*.

The experience with Ginny gave me insight not only into *her* difficulties but into the similar difficulties that many would-be pianists suffer. They may not have had such unfortunate childhood experiences as she, but I recognize the same glazed look when they try to decipher piano music. It is not hard to spot the ones who are still trying to keep "all those notes" straight in their heads. I realized that I had accidentally found a way around the problem sideways, both literally and figuratively, and the long view had opened up.

If you are a non-pianist, or one of the many pianists who never quite cracked the mystery of reading notes well enough to feel comfortable, you may be intrigued by now. I think I can make things clearer yet, even to a complete novice. So hang on, if you are curious about what has always seemed a complex system of reading piano music.

"Line-note" simply means a note written on a line: the line goes through the middle of the note. "Space-note" means a note drawn between lines. Each line and each space on the staff represents a particular white key on the piano keyboard. (Ignore the black keys for now.)

The names of all those 52 white keys are easy, for we use a repeating musical alphabet of seven letters, A B C D E F G, A B C D etc., starting with the first white key farthest to the left on the keyboard. Notice how the location of letter names is related to groups of black keys, which alternate between groups of two and three. (The single black key at the far left would be part of a group of three if the keyboard extended farther to the left.) Once you see that D falls between 2 black keys you can easily find *all* the D's on the keyboard, etc.

Now back to line-notes and space-notes. If you go from one line-note to the next line-note, you skip the space-note in between. Likewise if you go from one space-note to the next, you skip the line-note in between.

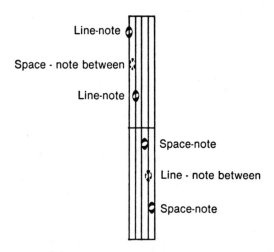

Look now at this arrangement of the "grand staff," which means the combination of two staffs of five lines each. We write notes from mid to high range on the treble clef   staff, and the notes from mid to low range on the bass clef ℐ: staff. If you have studied some piano you will probably associate treble clef   with the right hand, and bass clef ℐ: with the left hand, which matches our vertical diagram nicely. But we *can* use either hand, or both, to play notes in either clef. As a matter of  fact, take special note of the fact that in the following exercises you will use *both* hands in bass clef, and then both hands in treble clef.

On the diagram you will notice that the two staffs are separated by a space, and that there is a note drawn on a little short line between the staffs. That note happens to be a C, and is the famous "middle C" you keep hearing about. It's aptly named, for as you can see, with the two staffs lined up in relation to the keyboard, C rests smack-dab in the middle *between* the two staffs—but *not* in the exact middle of the piano, as you might have imagined. (Later we will pull treble clef and bass clef further apart, but it is important to see them this way first.)

96

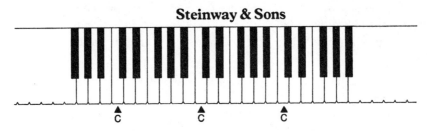

All C's look alike on the keyboard, for C always falls on the white key to the left of two black keys (*not three*). Try finding *all* the C's on the entire keyboard to orient yourself. Now find the C that is a bit to the left of center of the keyboard. That's middle C. With a pencil, mark an X on it. Don't worry about hurting the ivory or plastic key; the pencil mark will rub off easily.

Okay, now. Are you ready for action? Look at the following diagram:

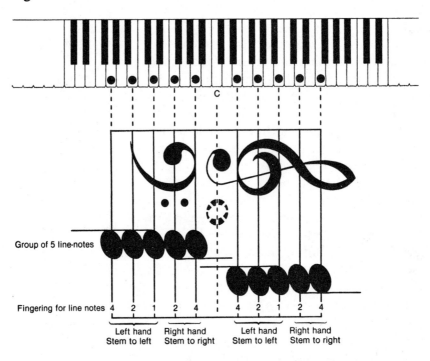

On the keyboard pick out the five line-notes to the *left* of middle C. These are your bass clef lines. Check the diagram carefully to be sure you have found the correct keys, then draw a pencil line on each of the five ivories. Remember that you must always skip a white key between line-notes to leave room for the space-note. Be sure that you leave middle C alone when you play this five-line group of notes. *It is not a part of this group* but is an important guide for orienting yourself on the keyboard.

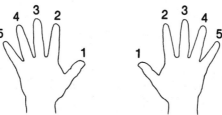

Play these five notes all at once, using the fingers indicated on the diagram. You will see a line called a "stem" connecting three notes and extending to the left; use your left hand to play these. The right hand will play the two notes with the stem extending to the right. Relax and enjoy the sound of those five notes. They form a beautiful chord.

Now do the same with the group of five line-notes to the right of middle C on the treble clef, again drawing five lines on the keys.

Play around with these two groups of notes until you feel perfectly comfortable with their location. To reinforce your instant recognition of where the groups are located on the keyboard, play each group and then look away while you drop your hands and shake them out. Better yet, get up and walk away from the keyboard to disorient yourself even more. See how quickly you can find the groups each time you come back to the keyboard. Now, to further reinforce your grasp of these groups, play the group of line-notes in the bass clef, and hold onto them while you *look* at the treble clef lines on the keyboard. Now move your fingers to the treble clef lines. Do the same thing in reverse: while you hold down the treble clef lines, *look* for the bass clef lines. *Then* move your fingers to the bass clef lines. When you can do all this easily, erase the lines you drew on the keys, and do it all again.

When you "look before you leap," orienting yourself visually to the other set of lines before you let go of the first set, you grasp more quickly the concept of the two staffs as they relate to each other and to middle C. They more quickly become part of one continuous diagram or map of the central part of the keyboard. With the line representing "C" invisible except when we actually need to use it, we get visual separation into two groups of lines which facilitates reading the notes.

When you are comfortable with the two groups of line-notes, five on each staff, you are ready to take a look at the four space-notes that lie between the lines. First play the five line-notes (in either bass or treble clef) and see the four space-notes raised up in between. Next move your fingers to these four notes. Use the second and fourth fingers of each hand (leaving out the thumb that you needed when playing the five line-notes). Check locations with the following diagram, noticing where the notes lie in relation to the groups of black keys.

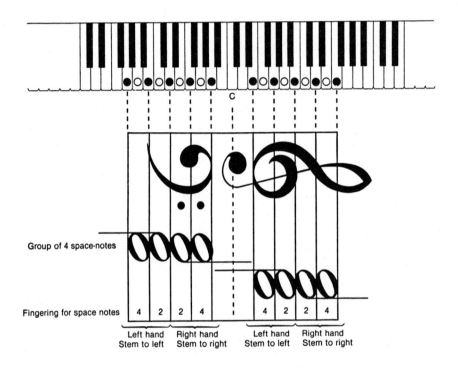

Go back and forth between treble clef and bass clef, playing these two groups of space-notes, four each, just as you did when playing line-notes. Close your eyes in between or leave the piano, just as you did when playing line-notes. Next, play the five line-notes in bass clef, and then shift to the four space-notes in bass clef. Do the same in treble clef. I keep re-emphasizing that there are *five* lines with *four* spaces between, because it seems to be a step that people often miss.

As soon as you're comfortable with the concepts, it's time to try out the short piece on the facing page if you have a keyboard handy. Don't be concerned with timing or rhythm. All we are after right now is an understanding of how the musical staff relates to the keyboard.

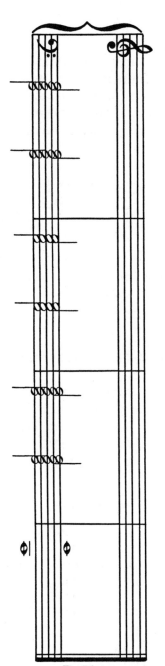
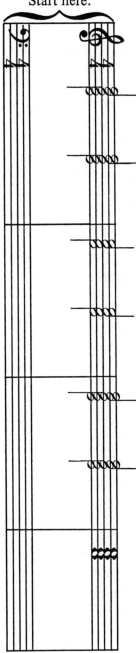

End here.

At the end of the piece there are notes written *off* the staff on short lines called *leger lines* (pronounced "ledger"). We can use these extra lines or adjoining spaces any time we need them, which puts an entire keyboard at our disposal. It obviously simplifies matters to use only our two five-line units as a base structure, for if we used all the lines possible on the keyboard we would have a total of twenty-six lines. Such a mass of lines would be totally confusing, whether vertical or horizontal.

All those other lines are still there and available. They are invisible except when we need them. When we do, we just grab a little segment of invisible line and make it visible, as we did earlier with middle C. If I want to wander off the staff to a note three lines to the right of treble clef, I draw in three leger lines and put a note on the third line (1). Or I can go to a note five lines to the right (2). I 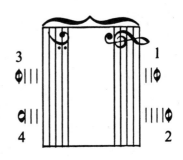 can write a note four lines to the left of bass clef (3), or on a space just left of the third leger line to the left of bass clef (4).

One more small point. If you look at the piece you tried and at any regular piano music, you will see that the treble clef and bass clef staffs are pulled farther apart from each other than in the diagram relating the staffs to the keyboard. That extra separation gives you the option of writing certain notes two different ways: either as they relate to treble clef or as they relate to bass clef. For instance, I can write middle C either one leger line to the right of bass clef, or one line to the left of treble clef (5). I can write the note E on the left line in treble clef, or write the same note in bass clef by adding two leger lines to the right (6). I can write A on the right-hand line in bass clef or by adding two leger lines to the left of treble clef. (7). In each of these examples, the two different notations refer to the *same key* on the keyboard.

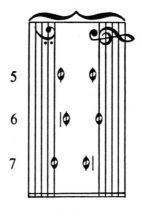

Now let's flip that grand staff into its usual position.

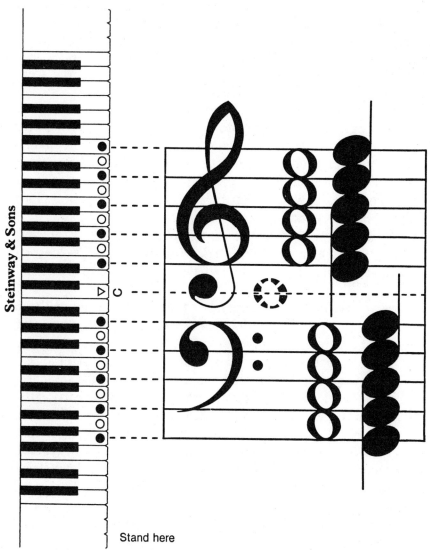

Stand here

Stand up at the far left end of the piano keyboard and turn side-ways, so you are looking along the keyboard, holding this book in front of you. Remember those black lines you drew on the white keys representing the grand staff? Mentally extend those black lines out into space a few feet. Can you imagine drawing a treble clef over the upper set of five lines and a bass clef over the lower set? Imagine writing notes on your staff. When you look at the staff this way, you can see that it still makes sense. This is, of course, the direction you have always seen the staff before. If you listen to the sounds of the piano, you will also notice that as the lines go up (away from you) on the staff, they go up in pitch, and as they come down the staff, they come down in pitch. Perhaps the way we conventionally write music does make some sense after all! When you sing, the conventional staff does indeed seem logical, for up in pitch is up on the staff.

It interests me that when I first published *Bold Beginnings* I turned only a few beginning exercises into the vertical position. Perhaps it's because the music looked so strange this way to me—despite finding out over and over that it does not look strange to a beginning student—that I could not bring myself to actually have the first five or six pages of pieces printed this way. Yet in using the book, I almost always turn the book sideways until a person has a firm grasp of the system. If someone leans toward dyslexia or certain other perceptual problems, they often keep the music turned sideways for several weeks—or even months—before it feels comfortable to turn the music back to its usual position.

It was a revelation to discover, after working for some time with the concept, that the vertical position makes sense not only to beginning pianists but also to certain people (such as Ruth, in Chapter 6), who have played the piano for many years but who never grasped the logical relationships in musical notation. I remember inadvertently spoiling a night's sleep for an acquaintance once. We met at a dinner party at the home of Ginny, the friend whose problems prompted this whole new way of looking at the keyboard. Mark told me with great chagrin that he yearned to play well but could never make sense out of reading piano music. He had just finished a PhD in math so I was not worried about any lack of intelligence. It was the old checkerboard-bumping again—someone with obvious brains feeling dumb because the teaching style hadn't matched his learning style during his several years of lessons. For want of paper and pencil, I drew creases in a napkin with a table knife to represent the lines of a staff, and started describing the connection to the keyboard. I spoiled his dinner as well as his night's sleep, for he got so excited about the concept that he forgot about his food. Later that evening we hunted up a piano to try out some more ideas, and later yet, when he went to bed, his mind kept whirling around with his new image of a keyboard connecting with a musical staff.

If you are curious, turn the page and you will see the first piece I wrote for Ginny that one memorable night when I flipped the staff over onto its side. It is printed here vertically—as I conceived it—rather than horizontally as it appears in *Bold Beginnings*. You know enough now to find the notes on the keyboard, and if you have an understanding of rhythm notation, you can add that also.

So there you are. Since you have an entire keyboard available to you, you might want to hurry off to the best piano teacher you can find and carry on! You have the long view—now you can again pay attention to the wild flowers near your feet and the lichens on the rocks for a while.

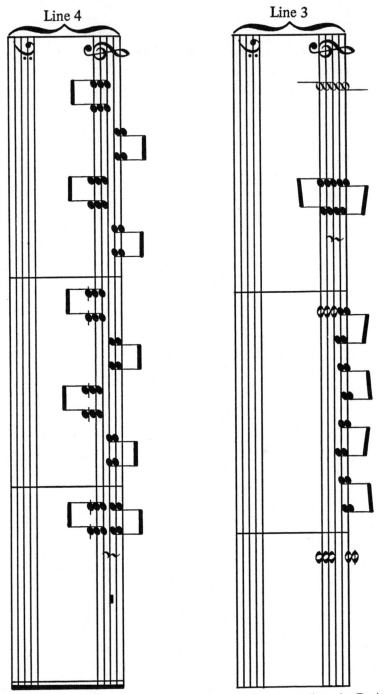

From *Bold Beginnings,* by Eloise Ristad. © 1968, 1975 The Mediaworks/Dorian Press, Box 1985, Boulder, CO 80306.

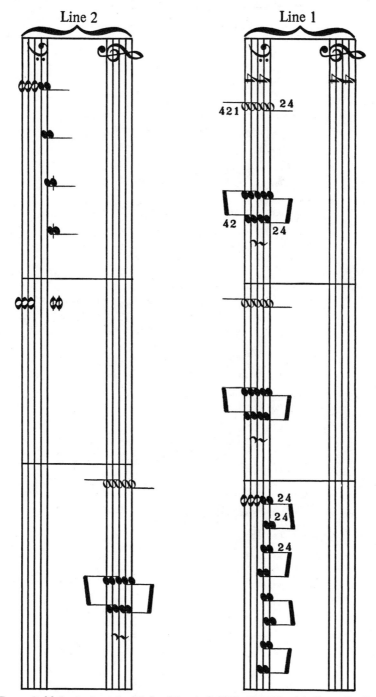

From *Bold Beginnings,* by Eloise Ristad. © 1968, 1975 The Mediaworks/Dorian Press, Box 1985, Boulder, CO 80306.

105

8. None of the Old Words Seem to Work

"I don't know what's wrong with me," said Susan Cable, a college piano teacher. "When I try to describe some of the things that have happened this week in the workshop, I just fumble around for words. It's as though I need a whole new vocabulary. None of the old words seem to work."

In the workshop Susan had been astonished to leave her familiar verbal world for another less familiar world. She had danced her pieces, she had turned her imaginative self loose, she had stood on her head with Liz, our soprano. She had shaken out her tidy concepts about Haydn and Chopin and Bach, and experimented in preposterous ways until she found subtleties she could never have planned. She had confronted her well-disciplined judges and sent them packing. She had listened to the child-within who knew how to fantasize and skip and romp. She had lost her reverence for old authorities and discovered a new inner source of authority.

And now none of the old words seemed to work. Perhaps she had entered territory where words are best left alone for the time being.

One of the participants in the same group was Larry Graham, the teacher/concert artist, who had spoken so eloquently against—but really *for*—the use of movement that one memorable day at lunch when he illustrated so graphically with his arms and body his response to a certain passage of music. He was still a skeptic, but a delightful one, for he was truly curious. He shared with the group his irritation with a baffling passage in the last movement of the Beethoven *Sonata in D Major*, Opus 10, No. 3. "I can never get what I want here, because it needs to be absolutely dead for several measures, then suddenly erupt. But I can never get it to be as dead as it ought to be."

I asked him what he meant by "dead," and why he felt it should be

107

that way. He wasn't quite sure, except that the passage was marked *pp*: pianissimo, very soft. His natural impulse was to play it with a lot of nuance and feeling. Yet he realized when he tried it that too much feeling too soon destroyed the impact of the later eruption of sound. He had a sense of having to *kill* that impulse to play it expressively. Perhaps this is how he got the idea that the passage should be "dead." He was caught again, as we so often are, by words that sounded right.

An interesting dilemma. I wondered out loud how it might feel to stand dead still, to get more of the sense he was wanting. We tried. Try it yourself, with eyes closed. . . . *Dead still.* . . .

Did you feel your shoulders and breath lock, your knees go rigid? Yet even as you forced the stillness, did you sense movement that could not be restrained? Now try it again, but this time let your body go *soft*. Breathe gently into the stillness. Sense the subtlety of movement throughout your entire body. Find out how that subtle movement enhances your sense of quiet and calm.

As the group experienced this, the stillness became an aliveness in the air around us. "Now anticipate an eruption of sound and movement. When the stillness has gathered enough force, let it erupt. But don't manipulate the eruption; let it come from the power in the silence." . . . The group sensed the gathering of force. Then, as though we were following an unseen conductor, we surged into a simultaneous crescendo of movement and sound.

Larry needed no coaxing to try this out on the piano. He no longer needed to superimpose a verbal concept on his playing. He no longer needed to bully his fingers into deadness. Just as there were subtleties of movement when we experimented with standing still, there were subtleties of nuance that intensified the sense of quiet in the music. The shadings were barely perceptible, yet created the suspense necessary for the later explosion of sound. Not only did the quiet section make more sense, the burst of sound also felt more convincing. His words had misled him about what was needed; his body had not.

"I'll be damned!" he said. "That's exciting, but you know, this whole movement frustrates me. I love the sonata except for this final movement. But it . . . well . . . I guess it embarrasses me to play it."

He tried to describe the nature of his embarrassment. "The piece starts out with a scrappy little ascending phrase only three notes long." He played it to demonstrate. "There's a pause, the short phrase is repeated, there's another pause, and then an extension into a longer statement. Each time the music really gets going it collapses again when this sequence returns."

Larry is one for long melodic phrases and lush nuances, so this stop-and-go business left him feeling as if he were riding on a subway train where the power keeps failing. There was no electricity in the pauses, which left the short phrases dangling limply each time they appeared, while he waited dutifully for the pauses to go by in between. When the music presented him with longer phrases he charged into them gratefully until the next interruption.

"Can you put into words what you want?" I asked.

"That's just the problem; I'm usually very clear on such matters, but in this particular spot I just can't figure out what Beethoven wanted."

"How about acting out the character of the music?"

He insisted it had no character at all, but humored me by trying. He half-hummed the bothersome three-note phrase, shook his head, then tried it a few more times before he began to find a quality he could act out. He surprised himself by discovering a mocking character in that little ascending phrase. His movement developed a *"Nyah, nyah, nyah"* quality to it that tickled his funny bone. We laughed as he poked fun at stuffy musicians present in his imaginary audience, and mocked imaginary pompous critics. He hammed it up so much that he lost any remnant of selfconsciousness. He actually found himself enjoying the pauses, which now vibrated with suppressed energy.

"Hey, I'm getting so carried away I almost forgot about the piano." The group picked up his mocking act as he went back to the keyboard. What happened in the middle of the piece was fascinating. The taunting irreverence in the ever-recurring sequence began to change into an insistent question, with the pauses now probing deeply within us. Larry also felt the change, and the power in his playing carried us along with him to new understanding of the music. It was impossible to tell whether his playing shaped our movement or whether our movement shaped his playing. It didn't matter. Together we discovered something that we might never have thought out logically with tired old words.

Yet when we came together afterward and talked about what had happened, words worked again. We had a different frame of reference, for we had all experienced something on a physical and emotional level that gave the words new meaning.

I was reminded of the first time I tried cross-country skiing and was given a *non-lesson* by a friend. She was apologetic about her lack of teaching ability, because she found it impossible to verbalize a set of instructions. She had skied for so many years that it seemed as natural to her as walking. That suited me fine, for I really wanted to get my own sense of the skis before I got tangled up in someone else's "how-to's." As I watched her push off in an elegant glide, I found that I could sense her rhythm in my own body. I watched, fascinated by the simple beauty of that glide. Then allowing the subliminal messages to my muscles to become real ones, I fell in behind her. My body felt resilient and light as I translated what I saw into what I felt. She stopped from time to time and tried to explain what she was doing with ski poles and skis and knees and legs and arms. I listened politely, but the real learning occurred when she took off again.

She was even more at a loss when we moved to a slope and started working on turns, a more complex task. Each time she tried to put the process into appropriate words, she would break off with an impatient gesture and say "Here, let me try it myself and see if I can figure out a better way to explain it to you." Off she would go, the rhythm in her body once again finding the better way to teach me before she ever got to the words.

She needn't have apologized. I was doing fine. At the end she even commented that I was already skiing like an old pro, but since she had no confidence in her nonverbal approach she suggested that I schedule a "real" lesson at the ski resort. I did, and it was temporarily my undoing. Immediately I got attached to the verbal instructions and lost the natural rhythm I had picked up so easily *without* words. When my head tried to take over, my body balked and got self-conscious and clumsy. Each time I fell I got more determined to keep things straight.

I worked my way out of my dilemma after the teacher left me on a downhill slope at the end of the lesson to practice my turns. Though the right turn was easy, my left turn was a mess. I was sure I remembered correctly what she had said about where to put the weight, which way to lean, which way to do what. But the "which way's" and the "where to's" would scramble themselves in my mind about mid-turn, and by the time I unscrambled them I was eating snow.

Finally I stood still, poised for a run and a left turn, and closed my eyes. With no verbal instructions, I simply visualized going downhill and turning easily to the left, feeling slight impulses in my muscles as I did so. As soon as I opened my eyes I took off. Beautiful! Why had I been making it so hard? It felt so good I wondered if it had been just luck. I tried it again. Eyes closed . . . a down-glide . . . a turn to the left. Then eyes open . . . down . . . to the left— on the real hill. "Aha, it wasn't just luck; my body is smarter than I thought." With what joy I connected a few months later with Denise McCluggage, who describes similar imaging in her fine book, *The Centered Skier.*

The next time I went skiing, I worked on my own, feeling free to experiment with those sometimes unwieldy, sometimes cooperative boards. The visualizing was a valuable tool, and brought me full circle back to verbal knowledge of what I was doing. By the time I had another lesson it was easy to assimilate new verbal instructions without leaving my intuitive wisdom behind.

Words. How easy it is to get lost in words. How often we drown in words when we try to describe even the simplest instructions or procedures. I know the feeling so well from writing and rewriting, time after time, Chapter 7 for this book. The hardest part of that chapter, of course, is the part teaching a non-pianist how the keyboard connects with a musical staff. It's hard for me because I know it *too well.* How do I describe in words something that is crystal clear to me, but unknown to a reader?

Whatever clarity I finally achieved came about only because of the many people who agreed to be guinea pigs. My requirement for such volunteers was that they be as innocent as possible of any prior knowledge of reading keyboard music, or that they be uncomfortable about it because of previous unpleasant experiences. "Don't blame yourself if it doesn't work," I warned each one. "Blame my writing."

When I was anywhere near, it took enormous self-discipline not to run in with a helpful hint or two if I heard someone struggling to understand what I had written. I learned to hand them the manuscript and leave, with only my written words to guide them.

The first few tries were discouraging. I found one man making soft tentative sounds on the keyboard that had nothing to do with what I thought I had written. He was happy, because he felt friendly towards the piano for the first time in his life. He thought that was enough to ask. I was far from happy, though, and did some determined rewriting. When I read the next draft I was pleased, thinking I had solved the problems. The next person got totally lost in the new verbiage, and despite my warning, he felt a failure. "No, no," I insisted, "it's my fault"—at the same time I was hoping that it was *his* fault. I tried it out on someone else just to be sure. She got lost, too.

Back I went to the typewriter, and back inside my head, to figure out how to get the right words down. Finally the words began to work in the way I had intended—actually saying what I *thought* they said all along. My volunteers no longer felt stupid, and I began to trust my intelligence again. I stopped drowning in the very words that were supposed to illuminate people.

Words also drown me when I get caught in what Frederick Franck in *The Zen of Seeing* calls "holy jargon," vague high-sounding words from which we *all* need a declaration of independence. That holy jargon becomes so familiar that I sometimes find myself in the middle of it before I realize what is happening. I have several friends who keep me honest when I start writing in vague, philosophical terms, dipping words in starch and ironing them onto the page, pretending that since they look so tidy they must have meaning. Take this sentence that I wrote just a few minutes ago for this chapter: "If we wish to understand more fully what life means, or how to answer life's great perplexities, we must be alert to each opportunity to invest words with new life."

It sounded and looked good when I wrote it, but as I reread it now, my brain floats off like a dandelion seed. I miss the simple message of how important it is to use words that connect directly with experience. And now that I've made this confession, I am wondering when my words will make *your* brain float off. If you have been conditioned by philosophical vagueness as much as I, I probably needn't worry too much. When I read jargon that has no precise meaning, either I read my own meaning into it, or I feel intimidated because I can make no sense of it.

I feel that one of the reasons the experiments described in this book work so well is that we get words out of the way momentarily. Ordinarily we do a lot of brain-stuffing when we try to learn anything. It feels refreshing to get rid of words long enough to stimulate other learning senses. I love the flash that comes when something clicks into place for me—when my longing to know suddenly becomes knowing. It is a moment of magic, created by my own thirst. The words that come after the fact seem charged with that same magic. They are the same words as before, yet not the same, for they have been brought back to life by the reality of an immediate experience.

Susan, who said "None of the old words seem to work" didn't really need a whole new vocabulary. She simply needed to let her experiences settle in until whatever was necessary trickled back into the word part of her brain. The essence of those experiences would remain apart, warming a deep mysterious core that has no word-squared boundaries.

9.
Meadowlarks,
Minds,
Muscles,
and
Music

I had a different spot planned for the story about the ski turn in the preceding chapter. I had planned to use the story as a way of introducing the value of visualizing. But my words took off on their own and I like where they went. I felt like I do when I leave the freeway for a stretch and make discoveries—a meadowlark that calls from a fence post just as I drive past, a twisting road that leads to the sea, a charming village that tourists haven't discovered, or maybe nothing but a roller-coaster country road that hasn't had the stomach swoops engineered out.

My friend, Peter, and I discussed the phenomenon of writing one day. He was in the midst of writing a novel and had discovered his characters developing their own identity in a most irritating way. His well-thought-out plot acted like the design in a kaleidoscope. The very act of writing jiggled the design and shifted it into new patterns. When he tried to hang on to his original plan for his characters, they pouted and balked and immobilized him at his typewriter. He had to stand aside and watch them in action before they would release his fingers on the typewriter again. It was like my left turn on the ski slope. I had to see it in action, and feel it in action, before it worked.

Eric Jacobson, a talented high school student who had recently won a national award in composition, was working on a set of pieces for woodwind quintet while studying with me. Five of the pieces had almost written themselves, with Eric coasting on the ego boost from his recent award. Not over-endowed with patience, he struggled for a couple of weeks trying to manufacture clever ideas for the last two pieces. He came in discouraged and tired of his unproductive efforts.

We talked a bit about the qualities of each of the first five pieces he had already written. One was frantic, one was playful, and so on.

115

Together we brainstormed a list of adjectives that might stimulate ideas for the remaining two. It was great fun, but did not spark his composing skills the following week.

Eric was unwilling to settle for five pieces in the suite and go on to a new project, so something needed to happen to end the deadlock. This was near the time that I discovered the value of visualizing in my skiing, and I had an inspiration. Why limit this to skiing? Why not apply it to composing?

"Close your eyes," I told Eric. "Put yourself in a concert hall and imagine that your set of pieces is being performed."

Together we created imaginary details about the musicians in his woodwind quintet—a freckled bassoonist with red hair, an oversized oboist who made the oboe look like a toy, an undersized flutist with blond hair piled on top of her head, a box-shouldered horn player with a lavender tie, and a fastidious-looking clarinetist. Eric chuckled as he watched his characters walk onstage and heard them play the pieces he had already composed.

"Hang on," I said. "The clarinetist is checking his reed and the horn player is dumping the moisture out of his horn. Okay, they're all set, ready to start number six. Are you ready?" Number six, of course, was not yet composed.

Eric listened intently, then opened his eyes and grabbed a pencil. "Unbelievable! I could really hear them playing it. What a great piece!" He scribbled down some quick ideas, then went back to his imaginary concert hall to see if his quintet would produce a finale to his suite. They obliged, and he grabbed his pencil again.

I was as excited as Eric—perhaps even more so—because the implications of what had happened were far-reaching. When I visualized a ski turn, I also felt the turn in my whole body. The term "visualize" is inadequate, of course, because it implies only *seeing*, while the sense of actual muscular impulses was stronger and more important than my visual image. When Eric visualized his quintet, his imaging again involved more than sight; in this case the sense of hearing was the key factor. While my image of the ski turn produced muscular sensations, his image of his quintet produced auditory sensations. In either case, we could follow the image with action.

If the visualizing or imaging worked that well for both my ski turn and Eric's composing, I wondered what the applications might be in cleaning up difficult passages in music that often seem erratic and undependable. Perhaps here, too, we get messed up because we don't have a clear image of the passage and thereby give ourselves too many conflicting messages about how to play it. I wondered how many senses would be involved. The visual sense would be necessary, both to see the music on the page and the consequent patterns on the keyboard or other instrument. Certainly hearing in advance would be important. What about the pre-sensing of muscular impulses that I had experienced in the ski turn?

It didn't take me long to find out, once I took my experiment to the piano. That sense of muscle involvement was indeed important; it was, in fact, the most important sense involved, both for me and for the students I experimented with in the next few weeks.

"But I don't know how to visualize," said one girl, and I realized that what seemed natural and easy to some of us was not as easy for others. Yet almost everyone, whether they realize it or not, spends a lot of time visualizing. We waken in the morning and immediately start visualizing a good deal of the action for the day ahead. We may see faces ahead of time, or sense presences. Our minds may go out to the car on a snowy morning to see if it will start; we do a pre-run of appointments or plans for the day. Much of this kind of internal thinking is probably only visual, although even here we may sense some bodily reactions ahead of time. As I visualize, my forehead may contract with anxiety, I may relax with a warm glow in anticipation of meeting a dear friend, or I may tense up over the hectic pace of the day ahead.

These responding impulses in our bodies can reproduce in advance, through only the tiniest of impulses, the feeling of the movements in skiing, in throwing a basketball, in playing a passage on the piano. Robert Nideffer, in *The Inner Athlete*, writes:

> For instance, right now, without actually engaging in the movement, attempt to get both the image and the feelings associated with kicking a ball. Notice how, as you carefully attend to each movement, you begin to actually use the muscles involved. You don't use them in a way that increases strength but in a way that helps your coordination and timing. (p. 189)

The use of the muscles is so minimal that it feels more as if you sense the firing in the muscles without any real movement. I keep searching for better words than either visualizing or imaging since they imply only sight. Sometimes I call the sensation that I experience a "feeling sense." I don't know if I like that term, either. It's too flat and dull for something so alive. I've tried "finger-sensing," "kinesthetic imagery," "muscular sensing," "muscle memory in reverse." None of the terms quite work. "Muscle memory in reverse" comes close, but it's too long for a convenient handle.

Whatever it is, this sense is different from just thinking about playing the passage. My hands lie quietly in my lap as I visualize, which is different from wiggling my fingers and playing the passage in the air. My internal rehearsal is different from playing a passage silently on the piano. It is not the same as just remembering what the notes are, because of that distinct sensation in the muscles. When I experience this "feeling sense" for a passage in music, I sense in advance exactly how the keys will feel under my hands on the keyboard, how the black keys and the white keys create a pattern under my fingers, how the stretches and contractions of my hands feel, and the sensations in my fingertips as they play. I don't think about any of this; I simply play the passage mentally, feeling all those tiny muscle impulses. The term "feeling sense" comes close, because I actually feel in my imagination.

In a group we sometimes play a sensing game that helps those who aren't conscious of their own ability to use this sort of kinesthetic awareness. We first make a guess as to how many steps it will take to walk from one side of the studio to the other. Each of us states our guess. Then with eyes closed, we mentally walk the distance and count the number of steps, kinesthetically feeling each step while standing still. Finally we actually walk the distance and count. People tend to be inaccurate when they simply state a guess. But when they visualize walking and feel actual impulses in their muscles—just as I did when I imaged the ski run—their estimate is apt to be far more accurate.

A graduate student in piano tried the experiment and grossly underestimated the number of steps, guessing that she could reach her destination in six steps. When she closed her eyes and mentally walked across the room feeling the impulses in her muscles, she came up with ten steps. When she opened her eyes and actually walked the distance, she made it in eleven. Many people who underestimate or overestimate when they guess, find themselves very accurate when they visualize.

"I wonder if that tendency to under-guess the number of steps is related to what happens in a long sixteenth-note run—like in my Mozart sonata. I often find things getting compressed in the middle of it. The notes get bunched up and my fingers can't quite keep track of where they are." She was a step ahead of me; this is the direction I was going with the exercise.

The problems did, indeed, seem related. She closed her eyes and imaged playing the troublesome run, sensing each note under her fingers, then opened her eyes and played a clean run.

"Amazing! Let me try that out on another passage that's even harder." She was disappointed when it didn't work.

"Was it absolutely clean in your imagination?" I asked. She admitted that it actually wasn't—that she had seen and sensed some of the same old bunchiness in the middle. She realized that whatever she sensed ahead of time, she played. The difference between imaging distinctly and imaging fuzzily is subtle. Our fingers are frustratingly accurate in using the information we give them. If we imagine sloppily, we play sloppily; if we imagine clearly and precisely, that is how we play.

She tried again, and found she needed to check the score to sharpen the accuracy of her imaging. When she was clear in her image and had the sense in her fingers, she found the same clarity at the piano. I told her about my experience on the ski slope. I had also found that if my imagery was faulty I was apt to make the turn wrong and fall; if my image was clear, the turn worked.

The others in the group were not convinced until they tried the imaging themselves. Even when it worked, a couple of them were dubious, for it seemed too easy. I could empathize. It seems to conflict with all we know about hard work and discipline and struggle. It seems almost easier to use a list of painful practice techniques and go on a high-powered, muscle-punishing binge of practicing. When I practice, I often have to remind myself all over again to rest my busy fingers by putting my imagination to work. "Tomorrow," I tell myself. "Right now I'm too pushed to take the time." I keep forgetting it's a time-saver! And if my pushy self wins, I push myself right into a jam.

This kind of visualization—or feeling sense—works the same for a string player, a clarinetist, a singer, a dancer, or an athlete. The muscular impulses are there, yet not visibly so. A string player feels impulses in her bow hand, in her fingers on the fingerboard, in her elbows and shoulders. A clarinetist senses the weight of his clarinet, how his fingers move on the keys, how his lips and tongue feel in producing the tone. It's impossible, of course, to describe in words what you will feel. Experiment and find out for yourself.

If you get stuck in the middle of a passage as you visualize, you find out how well you actually know it. Your head can insist that you know a passage, when in reality you are unsure somewhere along the way. Your body, which cannot be lied to, responds to that lack of information with tiny fits and tantrums in the muscles. No need to chastise yourself if you find fuzz-balls instead of notes in some spots; just go in and sweep them out with some solid information from the score. Now check it out—can you run through it in one clean sweep? No? Get a stiffer whisk broom. Try again with even more information. Beautiful! Open your eyes now and try it on your instrument. Ahh—that's more like it. No playing in the cracks this time. Close your eyes and visualize it again—clean, smooth, just the way you want it. The instant you finish, open your eyes and play it again. Go back and forth a few times between visualizing and actually playing, keeping the feeling of work and effort out of it. If the whole passage doesn't sound clean, break it down first into shorter segments that work easily, and then begin overlapping segments. Always start such work with only a measure or two rather than an entire difficult passage.

Go a step further. Play the passage on your instrument, but run your *feeling sense* of the passage a tiny notch ahead of your fingers. "Oooh, hey!" exclaimed a man struggling to keep his right hand on the black keys in the Chopin "Black Key" Etude. "It was almost as though the black keys came up to meet my fingers!" No more slipping and sliding, trying hard to keep in contact. Another person described the strange feeling of notes that *wanted* to be played. When you first try, you may catch only a fleeting sensation at first. The sensation is so distinct, yet elusive, that I find the verbal part of my brain stalling when I try to describe it. Try it; play around with it. Denise McCluggage calls this method "Instant Preplay" in her book, *The Centered Skier:*

> Think of the turn as already existing in space in its powerful eloquence and simplicity. All you have to do is see it, ski into it, and put it on . . . rhythmically, down the hill, shadowing with your flesh and blood body the vision that precedes it. (p. 89)

We have all been told as musicians to "think ahead." I suppose "thinking ahead" could conceivably lead to this sense of preplay, but for me it is quite different. Preplay is a sensation rather than a thought, and the gap between the feeling sense and the playing is infinitesimal. It feels like an almost mystical connection—one that would enable you to continually surpass yourself if you were to master it consistently.

As you work with this *feeling sense,* either before or during playing, you may discover some further benefits. We are all bothered by the inconsistency of our playing: one time we play a piece superbly, then for three times in a row we can't even get through a certain passage. In getting a kinesthetic feel in your muscles *before* you play, you automatically drop some of the extra muscle involvement that gets in your way. You begin to differentiate, to use only the muscles actually needed for the task. By playing immediately after you open your eyes, you coast on your body's new perception, which accounts for people's astonishment when they suddenly find a passage easier to play. If they try it again to find out whether it was just luck, the old muscle habits often have time to catch up, and they will probably decide it was, indeed, just luck. But if they continue to visualize with a feeling sense, muscle patterns actually begin to change and become more dependable, more repeatable, less erratic. I have seen the change take place in just a few moments, when the discovery of a new set of muscle responses is so welcome that the body almost instantly gives up its old patterns. I wish it always worked that quickly!

The trick is to *let* the body give up the inappropriate patterns without forcing it. When we give it that chance, we begin building a sensible choreography of muscle impulses that we can trust, while forcing only adds *more* useless tension. The consistency that we longed for and tried to impose begins to develop, for muscles find it easier to flow through a sequence when it develops comfort and ease. Our fingers lose some of the jumpy, nervous queasiness that means lack of differentiation—lack of separating the useless tension from the movement that we actually need to play.

Moshe Feldenkrais, an Israeli physicist who developed a remarkable approach called "Awareness Through Movement," carries the concept even further. He is keenly aware of the remarkable changes that can take place in our bodies through imagining an action. He demonstrates this not only through his own work with people privately, but also in enormous workshops where he badgers or cajoles two or three hundred people at a time into experiencing dramatic changes in their bodies. As you work with him you become aware of how grossly unaware most of us are of our bodies: of simple movements, of our breathing, of which muscles do a task. His exercises are slow-paced and time-consuming, but Denise McCluggage gives us a shortened adaptation of one that is fascinating to try:

In the Centered Skiing workshops we do an experiment to demonstrate how the good side can teach the bad side. I learned it from Will Schutz at a weekend workshop at Esalen. He said he got it from Moshe Feldenkrais. It might not be recognizable to either of them now. . . .

Stand up with your right arm held straight out in front of you about shoulder height. Now turn your body along with your arm as you sweep it to the right as far as you can go without moving your feet or bending your knees or waist. Sighting along your finger, make a visual bench mark on the wall to note how far you have turned.

Now unwind back to where you started. Put your arm down for a moment to rest. Then do the rotation again, this time noticing where your eyeballs are as you turn. Chances are they are in the far right corner of their sockets—leading the way for your head, shoulders, and hips as you turn.

Come back to the start again. Lower your arm for a moment, then make the turn again, only this time leave your eyes behind, i.e., direct them to the left corner of the socket as you turn to the right. It might not be easy at first. Do that rotation, separating your eye movement from your head movement, five times. (Lower your arm between rotations to allow your muscles to send their many mini-messages.)

Then do another series of rotations, this time leaving your hips behind, i.e., twisting them toward the left as you turn the rest of the body to the right. It's not meant to feel graceful. Do it five times.

After you've done all that go back and do the turn just as you did it the first time—eyes, head, and body twisting around along with your arm—and note where your finger is in relationship to your first bench mark. If the instructions have been clear, your new mark will be distinctly farther around than your first one.

What you have been doing, as I oversimplify it, is breaking up some customary, piggy-backing neural paths to and from the brain, and thus increasing your range of motion. It is a good exercise, by the way, to include in a pre-ski warm-up.

Now to transfer some of that learning.

With your left arm straight out this time, do Step One as before, turning this time to the left and making your visual bench mark at the far extremity of your turn. Return to the front and move no more.

Standing in place, without moving, run through *in your mind* the rest of the earlier instructions, doing to the left side what you did to the right. Visualize it clearly, leaving the eyes behind, leaving the hips behind. When you have run through it five times each way as a visualization, actually bring your left arm around and again check your bench mark.

If you are like the skiers in the workshops you will be vocally surprised at the result. Your rotation to the left will be as improved, if not more improved, than your rotation to the right. Your right side has taught your left side.

From *The Centered Skier* by Denise McCluggage, Warner Books, 1977, pp. 86-88.

If we accept the implications of Feldenkrais' work, we understand how visualizing can be so important in learning a skill. It has been proved many times that visualizing, or mental rehearsal, can improve accuracy in making free throws in basketball, improve swimming strokes, help a bowler increase his average. After reading a first draft of this chapter, Tarzan Honor, former All-American athlete, said "Of course, I know exactly what you mean." Practicing through visualization was old stuff to him, and accounted for many of the records he set in sports.

The same feeling sense that works so dramatically in visualizing, then playing, short passages of music can also be extended to learning entire pieces. Howard Waltz, a fine pianist and professor emeritus of the University of Colorado College of Music, learns much of his new repertoire with the aid of such practice, finding it far superior to learning at the keyboard alone.

Many years ago, Howard heard of a concert pianist who learned much of her new repertoire while traveling on trains. He was intrigued with the idea of reducing a bulky grand piano to a weightless, soundless image in his head, infinitely portable and infinitely accessible. Since he lives in an apartment house where long hours of audible practice would not be appreciated by his neighbors, the idea was doubly appealing to him. He started experimenting.

Earlier in his career, he was asked to compose a number of works for modern dance. Though not a dancer himself, he developed a profound sense of the relationship between physical gesture and musical gesture. This sense served him well as he developed his new approach to learning piano music. When he studied a new score, he instinctively felt the physical gesture in his whole body as well as in his fingers. He carried this sense from the mental practice in his apartment to the piano in his university studio, where he learned still more through his savoring of each actual movement and gesture at the keyboard. Back in his apartment he reinforced his mental imagery with his vivid memory of sensations at the piano. He finds that by going back and forth between the two modes of learning, he bypasses much of the stage where it is so easy to program in erratic, undifferentiated and irrelevant muscle impulses.

These erratic muscle impulses can get a dancer in trouble, too. A modern dancer showed me a difficult, fast-paced sequence of movements she was rehearsing for a concert. Halfway through she was breathing so hard I wondered if she could make it to the end. "I've simply . . . *got* to start . . . jogging and . . . bicycling to build up my . . . endurance," she panted as she finished. I wasn't convinced it was endurance alone that she needed. I let her catch half a breath, then while she was still panting, asked her to sit down and re-run the whole dance sequence internally and find every resting point she could. "There *aren't* any!" she objected, wondering why I was so unobservant.

"Okay, try something else first. Swing your arm out in front of you and up above your head. Let it swing back down, then up, down. . . . Keep going with it constantly in motion."

She tried. *What's she up to?*

"Now find out what happens each time your arm changes direction."

Jean grinned as soon as she discovered that luxurious point of rest, so unmeasurable in duration, at the end of each arc. She moved her arm up, down, up . . . as though the movement were a meditation, savoring each fraction of an instant of rest. She was more than ready for her assignment when she stopped. She sat with eyes closed. I watched the corner of her mouth flicker many times as she discovered resting points in her dance that were "not there." When she had finished her first real run-through that morning she was exhausted, yet she got up silently now and danced through the whole sequence again. This time she was exhilarated and far less winded when she finished. Each change of direction had furnished her with a small resting point, and the dance had lost some of the frantic look it had before. There were still places in the dance, though, where she was working needlessly hard. This effort detracted from the sense of energy in the piece. I asked her to try her leaps—first by imaging and then for real. In her imaging I asked that she not worry about how she got up in the air or even if she *did* get up, but just to sense the luxury of gravity as she came back down to the floor.

She didn't argue this time. She was ready and eager. When she finished imaging, she opened her eyes and without a word launched into her leaps. "It's crazy," she said, shaking her head in amazement. "I swear I went higher, and came down lighter!"

Not crazy at all. The craziness is in the fact that we are astonished each time we discover that our minds and bodies work together in wondrous ways if we but give them the chance.

10.
Drink Your Milk; Don't Drink Your Milk

"Drink your milk." How often have we heard it. How often have we said it. "Milk is the perfect food. You can't survive without it."

"Milk may be damaging to your health." "Cow's milk is the culprit. Stay away from it." "*Don't* drink your milk."

What? Did I hear right? Not drink milk? You must be wrong.

How often it happens. You accept something as truth for your entire life, only to have some infuriating magazine article suddenly shake you to your toenails by stating that the reverse is "truth." "It isn't fair" you protest. You don't even want to hear it. You have been told that jogging is the way to perfect health: a healthy body, healthy heart, healthy lungs, healthy everything. Just when you finally break through a lifetime of lethargy and discover the intoxication of jogging, you read that jogging jars your entire skeletal structure, causes shin splints and ankle spurs, and creates a dangerous addiction. You follow your doctor's advice and carry lemon drops with you to keep your blood sugar up and energy level high, only to read that sugar causes your depressions and bad temper and sends your blood sugar down instead of up.

These are medical controversies that are at least theoretically resolvable when all the evidence is in. For the conscientious musician, however, controversy between teaching methods is not even theoretically resolvable. "The evidence" can prove almost anything. One book on technique is totally convincing. The next book is just as convincing, but unfortunately tears down every theory in the first book and leaves us hopelessly confused. One teacher advocates high finger action on the piano for good technique, and it really works. The next teacher has a system with fingers low and curved that requires a minimum of effort, and it also works wonderfully well and helps you get rid of the problems you developed with the high-finger technique. Little by little you become re-educated and convinced. That would be okay if you didn't make the mistake of going to a master class taught by a pianist who plays with flattened-out fingers and who gets a marvelous sound at the piano and uses a different approach that doesn't vaguely resemble either the high-finger technique or the "keep your fingers close to the keyboard" approach. You are absolutely devastated, but the sound is exquisite. How could you doubt a master pianist such as he?

So where does that leave us, pray tell? Surely there is someone we can put our faith in, and then stick with our beliefs. But there is always that little thread of doubt hanging off the hem of our belief system, and we can't seem to pull it out cleanly enough not to start another thread raveling. And life, not to mention piano technique, or violin technique, or snare drums or bag-pipes, is so full of those bothersome ravelings of doubt that it hardly seems fair. There *must* be a right way. There must be a right *way*.

It's no use. The suspicion still hangs around that someone else may have the truly right answer and that we will be found out to be an authentic fraud and be banished from the kingdom. The stronger the suspicion, the louder we become in our game of blind-man's-buff, promoting our own beliefs.

Perhaps this is why the whole authority-based system of teaching music, or any other skill, is so prevalent. It is scary to realize that there are many, many right ways, and that as we grow and develop, our perceptions change and shift about right or wrong ways. If we allow ourselves to become authorities, we tend to lock ourselves into the corner we label "right," and forget that every corner has its own share of rightness. If we pretend that only one corner is right, we must also pretend that we are not pretending. But we are free to explore each corner, one at a time, as well as the spaces between. We discover that some corners have resonance for us at certain times, and that we can move through and beyond the spaces that have no resonance to offer.

The Quakers have a lovely phrase: "What thee said spoke to my condition." And Quakers have no qualms about tuning out what is said in Meeting that does *not* speak to their condition. I sank gratefully into the luxury of that choice the first time I attended a Quaker Meeting, remembering the years of growing up in a traditional church where I felt duty-bound to listen attentively to the minister's every word. Somehow my drifting off during church had always seemed one of the sins of my life. Non-listening seemed okay when I was still young enough for my mother to give me permission to read the Sunday-school paper as long as I didn't rustle the pages. But there came that inevitable time when I knew I was too old to sneak a look at either a Sunday-school paper in my hands or the numberless pages of fantasy I always had available in my mind. Yet my mind would still sneak off, only to return with a start and wonder what on earth the minister had just been booming on about so earnestly. What if someone asked what I thought about the sermon? Even now if I attend a high-powered lecture and a speaker verges on a certain kind of evangelical thundering of his brand of truth, I automatically retreat into a soundproof cocoon and wait it out.

Yet there *are* speakers who "speak to my condition" from the moment they stand up, before they have spoken a word. When they speak, their words tug at my insides, and I know that it is the speaker's truth speaking to my own truth. It's like a spark jumping a gap between two wires.

The experiences and admonitions that don't speak to our condition are best recognized as drains on the energy we need for living. We often spend untold quantities of energy, first in trying to listen and stuff into our heads all these assorted theories on piano technique or staying healthy or investing our money, and second in feeling guilty that we somehow didn't manage to. Our bag of mismatched beliefs gets bulky and unmanageable, but it takes courage to dump it all out and find that in addition to one workable fountain pen and a blank pad, there are only three rubber bands and a couple of paper clips that are worth saving.

"Whew! Where did all that other stuff come from? How long have I been carrying this around?" We breathe a sigh of relief and start stuffing our bag anew. But the lightness lets us breathe some fresher air of our own choosing, and we drop some of our compulsiveness in filling our bag. As we shop the vast supermarkets of ideas and theories and recipes for success, we must discover through our own successes and blunders exactly what it is that works for us at this particular moment, and what we can use from the expert.

As a teacher, I sometimes delude myself into thinking I am speaking to a student's condition, when in reality I am only responding to an old compulsion to teach a certain thing at a certain time—to stuff certain truths into each student's bag. When suffering from such a delusion, I can also delude myself into thinking the student has learned what I thought I taught.

I remember a junior high school group coming in for a lesson and warming up together on scales. I spotted one of them fudging on the fingering when she came to the B♭ scale, and I threw a fit.

"Well, I just can't remember the fingering for this one. It always bugs me."

"Can't remember?" I echoed. "You're not *supposed* to remember. That's the last thing I want any of you doing—trying to *remember* your scale-fingerings." I have old memories of my teacher writing scale-fingerings in my lesson-book and admonishing me to memorize them. I take great pride in having students understand scales in terms of comfort and ease rather than in terms of arbitrary dictums to be followed and hated.

"How else am I supposed to know them if I don't memorize them?" asked Dot innocently, while I groaned.

"Look, we have talked several times just recently about scale-fingerings . . . or did I dream that?" I asked the other students.

No, I hadn't dreamed it, and yes, Dot had been there. There was a new student in the group who was fascinated by this new concept that his own fingers could figure out a fingering that worked. We had discovered again that some scales have only one very obvious fingering that is based on the fact that long fingers are comfortable on the raised black keys, and the thumb is happiest on the lower white keys. We had discovered that several other scales could be fingered comfortably in at least two different ways that were equally good, and that good old C Major, which is supposedly the easiest scale of all, since it is all on white keys, is actually the most difficult. The *supposedly* supposes the wrong thing, as is so often the case in anything as slippery as learning. The bland, innocuous C Major scale has no black keys to break up the landscape and give fingers some obvious point of reference. Thus this scale has any number of fingering possibilities that someone could decree as right. I had been happy about that session, because the new student, at least, had captured a sense of the elegance of scale-fingering and had dropped his old aversion to practicing scales.

Back to Dot, who despite all that, was still thinking scale-fingerings were absolutes, either to be memorized or rebelled against.

"Maybe she forgot the rule—the one that helps you remember the fingering on the scales that start with flats" said another student, wanting to make me feel better. I groaned even louder with that one. At this stage of the game I had a student who thought I was teaching them *rules* to remember? It was even harder to face when I realized that the rule she thought she remembered was wrong! And when she tried the rule, she messed up her own scale which had been going beautifully until she got selfconscious about remembering a possible rule.

"And you're my great, sophisticated junior high group that I take such pride in?" I moaned. "I thought I was finally learning to teach in a way that makes sense, and now you disillusion me like this!"

"Where did I go wrong?" I asked—the classic question we always ask as teachers or as parents. As soon as I heard myself, I said it again, this time melodramatically wringing my hands and looking upwards. I got a laugh and we went on.

"Well, you see," said one, "we have to remember rules so many other places that we forget you don't really teach that way."

Nice try, but I thought they were letting me off the hook too easily. We reconstructed one of the previous sessions when I had helped them through to the understanding I was aiming towards. It's a curious thing, but in that particular set of scales the fourth finger of the right hand tends to land on $B\flat$ no matter where the scale begins, while the fourth finger of the left hand tends to land on the fourth *note*. It's a convenient coincidence, and does indeed turn up in theory books at times as a *rule*. It's a perfectly benevolent, helpful rule, only I honestly didn't mean to teach it as a rule. Yet, in retrospect, I could clearly hear myself saying "Remember now . . ." as soon as the students happened on the discovery. Right there it became a rule to them. Why couldn't I trust the discovery itself? Why couldn't I trust the re-discovery if it were needed? The original insight spoke clearly to the students. But "Remember what you discovered" meant *right way*; "right way" meant *rule*; "rule," for Dot, meant *protect yourself and space out*. Even now as we talked, I saw the "down-the-street-and-around-the-corner" look in her eyes, and I knew we weren't finished.

The episode sparked a great discussion on the nature of learning and the nature of teaching that none of us will ever forget, and that would have done credit to a graduate seminar on learning theory. The kids were as fascinated as I with what we were discovering, and just as curious about the process that goes on when someone thinks he is teaching something and isn't, or when someone underscores a discovery and hammers it into a rule.

Dot finally confided to us her aversion to scales and that she would do anything to get out of playing them for her previous teacher. "I hated learning all those stupid rules about where the fourth finger goes in which scale. I could never remember where or why. I guess when we got to that fourth finger business in here I just automatically spaced the whole thing out. Sometimes I would pretend to pay attention long enough to make you think I had it so we could go on to playing Brahms."

"I can't believe how simple this scale really is," she went on. "It's even sort of fun." We had asked her to take a few minutes to experiment with all the different ways she could find to play the scale and find one that she really liked. It took less than a minute, for she was finally curious enough to find her own truth. Not content now that she had cracked that one so easily, she tried the E♭ scale, then A♭ and D♭. She would play one, then another, then go back to B♭. She was so absorbed that she didn't realize we were all watching.

"Hey, guess what I just discovered" she said as she turned to us and described a pattern that was emerging for her. Her pattern had nothing to do with fourth fingers, and seemed vague and imprecise to us. However, it worked for her. She now had a clear sense of those scales under her fingers. Her fourth fingers landed precisely where ours did, but that was not *her* way of guiding herself.

At times it seems as if it would undoubtedly be easier and quicker just to give students information and formulas and expect them to learn them. I'm often tempted to write in the fingering for a passage, for instance, rather than to take a chance on a student messing it up through discovery. Yet if I turn a group of students loose with a difficult passage to finger and actually leave the studio for a few minutes so I won't be tempted to interfere, they usually solve the problem admirably. They not only learn how to finger that particular passage, they also learn how to experiment and develop a fingering for other passages they encounter. If they are totally baffled by a portion of the passage, then they welcome my help. But if I first take the passage and arbitrarily finger it for them, they will almost invariably rebel during the week and come back with some kind of mess. This mess is usually so well-practiced that it takes weeks to unlearn.

If the student is part of the process of discovery—finding a fingering that works well, finding how important a flexible wrist is, discovering how to keep an arm relaxed on octaves—the solution to a problem then becomes a personal triumph. The solution becomes a self-given gift—a gift that means a welcome short-cut in learning this wonderful new piece. Because of that gift, the student is then more ready to accept the gift of my additional insight, or the insight of someone else in the group. Gifts that come only from outside sources not only make us lazy, but also resentful and rebellious. The gift of a teacher's wisdom too freely bestowed becomes a burden.

I recently taught a university course entitled "Principles of Piano Teaching." The fact that I had been hired on the basis of my unconventional approach to teaching not only bolstered my confidence but also put demands on me to live up to some rather vague expectations. My inner judges lined up and reminded me that I had never taught such a class before, I had never taken such a course myself (no comfortable old-shoe format to fall back on), and furthermore that I usually avoided reading books on piano pedagogy. On the other hand, it was a one-year visiting assignment, which meant that I was free to experiment without worrying about whether I would get rehired.

I had purposely prepared no course outline or reading lists so that I wouldn't box myself—or my students—in. But for all my brash self-confidence, I felt a little naked that first day facing students who expected an outline of the course they had signed up for.

"What's this course going to be like?" a student fired at me before I even had a chance to look at each new face. It was a legitimate enough question, but in the preceding hour I had been struggling with a young woman assigned to study piano with me, who was unhappy that I was insisting on working with piano students in small groups rather than individually. Since she was also in this class and still radiating offended vibrations, I felt I should watch my step before I managed to antagonize a whole class.

But before I had a chance to monitor my response I heard myself saying, "I don't know."

Startled looks. They all had notebooks open, waiting for a course description I didn't have. *Drink your milk* or *Don't drink your milk.* They wanted that certainty from me, or thought they did.

"You see, since I don't know any of you yet—your personalities, your backgrounds, whether any of you have done any teaching yet— how could I know ahead of time what the course will be like?"

Puzzled looks this time, but interested.

"What I do know is that I am not going to teach anyone in here how to teach."

Startled looks and puzzled looks turned into "Look, lady, why are you here?" looks.

I realized that I at least had their attention.

"We will have some experiences together here that may alter some of your perceptions of yourself and of teaching and of the world around you." *Heavens, where did that jargon come from?* Nobody but me noticed it was jargon. "We will share what we already know and explore some things we don't know." *Not much better.*

"Oh, come on" I plunged in, pulling up a chair and sitting down. "Nobody ever teaches anyone else how to teach, so let's not pretend. You learn how to teach by opening up, by questioning, by doubting, by exploring, by rebelling. You learn how to teach by learning how to learn.

"Tell me something. Take a moment to figure out exactly what happens when you learn something." . . . They found it hard to pin down.

"Take another moment and figure out what gets in the way of your learning. No, I don't want any answers yet," I said as a couple of hands shot up. "I want you to close your eyes and scratch around a little."

The request was so unusual that a couple of them could not force their eyes shut. Perhaps they felt exposed and vulnerable because of the silence I was imposing on them. I talked them through their inner journeys with more questions. Under what conditions do you learn best? . . . What physical sensation do you get when you learn? . . . How about when you resist learning?

"How surprising," said one student as she opened her eyes and the room came back into focus. "I had some ready answers until you asked us to close our eyes. Then everything went blurry and I realized what a mystery learning is."

"It was the opposite for me," said another. "When you asked us to figure out what gets in the way when we are learning, I hadn't the faintest idea. But almost as soon as you told us to close our eyes, I knew it was *me*. I'm the one who gets in my own way."

There were more responses, and I knew the class was on its way. Some were curious, some were touched in some inner part of themselves, and some thought maybe this would be an easy two hours of credit without the usual assignments of busywork. We lost the suspicious young woman who had such an instant aversion to my strange approach. But we gained some new converts to strangeness during the course of the year, and on the last day we had a picnic and tears and laughter while we shared some of the insights we had gained during the year.

How did they fare without any prescriptions for teaching, without formulas for learning, without some "basic concepts"? Some thrived and blossomed and left the air in the classroom tingling. A few would have fared better—on the surface, at least—in a no-nonsense methods class. But I like to think that even those few carried away a few tiny seeds of doubt about "right answers," "right teaching methods," and "right definitions."

One day I asked them to define the word "rhythm," since they would soon start teaching a group of seven-year-olds in the lab portion of the class. One by one they bit.

"It's a regular kind of pulsing," offered one.

"No, no, you're talking about a beat. It gets broken up if it's a rhythm," argued another.

"Broken up?" someone asked. "In what way?"

"Well, notes are different lengths."

"We haven't defined 'notes' yet," someone remembered.

"A note is a sound."

"No it isn't. A note is a *symbol* for a sound."

"Okay, then, rhythm is sounds that are different lengths."

"No, that doesn't do it either, because those sounds have to be organized in some way."

"Okay. You start out with a meter—"

"What's a meter?"

"I give up. This is hard."

"A meter is slightly longer than a yard," joked someone, as though things weren't confused enough already.

"Skip the meter business. Start out with a pulse—a regular rhythmic beat. No, I don't mean rhythmic, because that's what we're trying to define. Start out with a steady beat, then subdivide it in different ways and you get a rhythm."

"How are you going to teach that definition to seven-year-olds when we start teaching them next week?"

"How about drawing a pie and dividing it up?"

"What does a *pie* have to do with anything?"

"Or we could use an apple and cut it up into pieces."

"My teacher used to do that and I never had the foggiest idea how it connected with 'One, and-a two, and-a three.'"

I hadn't said a word since I threw out the question. But now I asked them all to push their chairs back and stand in a circle with their eyes closed.

"Find a pulse that feels close to your heartbeat. Don't struggle to find it; just take your time until you find a pulse that feels natural and right."

When I sensed that they were ready, I asked them to show that pulse in some subtle way with their bodies.

"Now open your eyes and add a soft clap to the movement. Without consciously either changing or resisting changing your own pulse, listen for a common pulse to emerge."

One joker in the group made his clap hard and solid to try to undermine the experiment, but even he yielded at last as a group pulse gently took over.

When the pulse was unshakable, I asked them to carry the pulse around the room, and from time to time to add rhythm to it. "Let the rhythms develop out of your body movements instead of thinking them up."

A fascinating rhythmic dance developed. "Hey, we're finally defining rhythm," someone realized, and drummed away on a passing pair of shoulders. They didn't want to stop, because they were releasing all the pent-up frustration they had felt when trying to deal with a verbal description.

I wished afterwards that I had had the patience to wait until their frustrations led them to a similar experiment with movement. But my own frustrations got the better of me when time began to run out.

Early in the course they asked what books they should read about piano teaching. With a perfectly clear conscience I steered them away from the many fine books on the subject and towards such books as *How Children Fail* and *How Children Learn,* by John Holt, *Teaching as a Subversive Activity*, by Neil Postman and Charles Wiengartner, *The Inner Game of Tennis*, and *The Centered Skier*. I felt the students needed to stir up a thousand-and-one questions of their own before they were secure enough with their doubts to be exposed to a thousand-and-one answers. So we held off from the obvious pedagogy books while they kept "inner game" logs of performances and practice sessions and explored their own learning from the inside out.

They became adept at asking questions that have no easy test-score answers. They learned much from the seven-year-olds who thought *we* were teaching *them*. Most important, they began to trust processes of growth rather than formulas. Their assignments became their own responsibility, as did their grades, with a clear understanding that assignments and grades and tests often have little to do with discovery and learning.

One young woman knew clearly by mid-year that she must resist the temptation to read any of the available books or articles on piano teaching and deal instead with her own confusion. I, as teacher, was delighted with her confusion, for she had begun the year with a dangerously glib system of beliefs about teaching. By the end of the year her confusion had changed into openness and an eagerness to explore her own wisdom and intuition. She had graduated; now it was safe for her to read anything she wanted to read, and to be exposed to any belief system. This was true not because she had been indoctrinated to the point that she could not be shaken from her own system, but because she had found that you cannot adopt any system without sacrificing the integrity of your own internal source of wisdom. At the time of soul-searching, when students decided on their own grades, she asked for an A for her journey through confusion. Another student asked for a lower grade, because he realized he had piled stacks of words into a dusty corner of his brain without finding the rich nourishment possible from them. He found that dutiful reports on what he had read had little of the joy that we all shared when we discovered how effectively our seven-year-olds could teach each other when we furnished them with the raw materials of learning, or when we discovered that the seven-year-olds were teaching *us*. Book-seaching for ideas on interpretation had little of the excitement that we found when we discovered the inner sense of a Brahms passage by dancing it. Books on technique seemed dull in comparison to solving the technical problems in a Chopin Ballade by free-wheeling experimentation.

A doctoral student in the class who had been "living by the book" in his own teaching, came to have a real sense of humor about his ready store of pat answers, and about his addiction to right answers from authorities. He would catch himself in mid-sentence asking me for the right answer to a problem in technique or interpretation or teaching, and then grin in relief when he realized that if I took the bait and imposed my version of truth upon him, it would rob him of finding his own version.

Before he finished his doctorate, he read many more books on piano pedagogy, on style, on technique. But he became more and more capable of saying "Hmm, interesting," and going off to experiment on his own.

"Hmm, interesting." I hope I can remember that the next time *I* need to say it.

11.
Maybe
I
Should
Just
Keep
Bees!

We sat on the floor with Cecily one day in a workshop. Cecily was scattered and distracted when she walked in, worried about not having anything to perform. "I'm so far behind in my work at school," she apologized, "and things are really getting out of hand at home."

She was in the last weeks of a master's degree program in fine arts, and had taken the workshop to alleviate the tension and get some fresh insights. A singer as well as an artist, she figured that if the singer relaxed a bit, the artist would be able to finish some dangling projects. She carried on a monologue that went something like this: ". . . and I have two more papers to finish that I haven't even started. . . . I *should* go with Sarah to her violin recital tomorrow. . . . Robert was probably just being kind when he said he liked my emerging concept in the sculpture, because I know how super-critical he is. . . . That last painting was a mess; I should have realized it was finished and not added that last splotch of magenta. . . . No matter what else happens, we *have* to celebrate Damon's birthday Tuesday. . . . I must buy Thomas some new shirts before he flies to Chicago next week. . . . Whoever is going to shampoo the dog before Mother arrives? . . . I haven't had a decent singing practice for weeks. . . ."

We could understand the frustrations she felt in juggling several demanding worlds, and as we listened we found ourselves sitting almost as hunched up and tense as she. She scrunched deeper and deeper into herself, with her forehead following the scrunch. Suddenly she blurted out, "Maybe I should stop it all and just keep bees!"

She spoke with great vehemence and intensity. Yet all of us, including Cecily, exploded with laughter. When we had spent ourselves with toe-tickling, rib-exhausting laughter, we looked at each other with the shy tentative feeling that follows such spontaneous abandon.

With the tension broken, Cecily acted out her worries in a different way, alternately taking the role of herself and of a demanding, unpleasant judge.

You're basically lazy; you need to work harder.

"But I'm tired of working hard."

Everything is falling apart. You're neglecting the kids and there's bound to be a crisis.

"I know. I can see it coming."

Those papers are still waiting to be done. Why have you put off writing them for so long?

"I just can't get into a creative frame of mind."

Excuses, excuses. What's your excuse for fading out on your commitment to the P.T.A.?

"That's the least of my worries right now."

The least of your worries? Fine model of commitment you are for your kids. And what about your voice lessons? You shouldn't have started them if you couldn't find time to practice.

"I was worrying about that, but my teacher understands the pressures I'm under."

You know you're stuck on your sculpture project and you didn't admit it to your advisor.

"I didn't want him ranting and raving at me. I'll think of something."

You're just running out of imagination. You'd better get your act together and be more responsible.

"I'm sick of getting my act together and being responsible."

You're acting like a child.

"Maybe I *want* to be a child."

What emerged was a saucy, impudent child who stuck out her tongue with a "so there." Once again laughter broke the tension.

We liked the spirit of this child, for she was ready to reclaim some of the rightful territory usurped by the judge and his cohorts. The judges fled in disarray, for they fare poorly in the face of spunk. Twice they had been routed—once by a beekeeper, next by a child.

Cecily flashed grateful recognition to her child-self; she had almost forgotten that part of herself. This child part had suffered over the past weeks, and needed some of Cecily's attention. In her fear of neglecting her children, her husband, and her academic work, she had grossly neglected this inner child. In blocking this impudent spirit, she also blocked the creativity that she needed to finish papers and art projects. As she talked with her judges, her tone lightened, and she played the alternating roles with more and more energy and flair. Nothing really changed in her life during those moments; the life-size demands were still there, the pressures were still real. Yet everything changed. She could stick her tongue out in glee and get those damned judges off her back, at least for the moment. She was once again free to be human.

Of course the next few weeks would be rough. Of course the kids would feel neglected for a while and her husband might have to buy his own shirts and the P.T.A. might suffer. But the family would survive and even make some significant discoveries in the process. The P.T.A. would find someone else to chair the bazaar. The voice teacher would be patient, and Cecily would soon get back to her singing with enthusiasm and joy. Already she had a flash of new direction on the stalled sculpture project. The papers to be written were not as ominous as before. For the moment, at least, she was free from the need to be a super-person.

I saw Cecily a few weeks later, and knew by her posture and attitude that the beekeeper and the child were alive and well. There were inevitable times when her judges had edged up to scold and nag and divert her. There were, indeed, minor crises in her family. But the beekeeper and the child could visit whenever invited, bringing with them the weapons of gentle humor and laughter.

As the rest of us participated in Cecily's drama, we were struck by similar dramas in our own lives. The need to be a super-person is an affliction that strikes many of us. Though this was not the warm-up I had planned for the session, we found we were all in the mood for further work. Since Cecily was not prepared to sing, we tackled a problem that Anne, another aspiring super-person, had brought to the group.

Anne was an actress as well as a musician, and had the lead in a play in a near-by city. She described a difficult scene toward the end of the play. She had a fast costume change, then, within minutes of her entry, she walks across the stage, finds a bundle of clothes belonging to her soldier son, and realizes that he is dead.

"Each time I walk on in that scene I worry about whether I will have to fake it again. It's terribly important for me to be sincere. You see, the whole play can be ruined in that one moment if I'm not convincing when I suddenly see John's hat and clothes and know he's dead."

We designed an experiment. "Play the scene for us; here's a hat you can use. But instead of trying to be sincere, play the scene like a melodrama. Let it be as overacted and phony as possible."

"I don't know if I can," objected Anne, appalled at the thought. But she shrugged and laughed, intrigued. "Okay, here goes."

She gasped and clutched at her heart in true melodrama fashion, then walked across the room to pick up the hat. Something happened the instant she touched the hat, and we were in tears during the rest of the scene.

Anne played the scene out, and sat down. We were silent as we pondered what had happened. When we could talk again, Anne said wonderingly, "But I really *did* try to make it a melodrama."

We knew. We knew she had tried, this time, *not* to make it sincere. How had it happened? What part of Cecily was caught unawares and played the part with so much power?

On the surface, the explanation was simple. Anne gave herself permission to be phony in the scene, even to ham up the phoniness, and suddenly the scene became real. When she stopped *trying* to be real, she was transformed into a flesh and blood, heart-thumping, real woman who had lost a son and was showing her grief.

How can the permission to be phony produce sincerity? What contrary streak in our nature responds in this way? Are we still just kids rebelling at Mother telling us to make our beds, to be good, to be nice to the company?

"Play a caricature of a bad sight-reader," I told a self-proclaimed bad sight-reader later that same day. He loved this role, after so many years of struggle to force himself to sight-read better. He played the role with great relish, yet found that the permission to be a bad sight-reader changed something. The notes on the page became more comprehensible when he tried *not* to read them accurately. His sight-reading problems were not instantly cured, by any means, but much of his panic disappeared.

"Forget about playing that passage without mistakes," I told another pianist. "Just watch your fingers make the mistakes." How often have I tried that trick since then! It almost invariably helps clean up a messy, overpracticed passage, often to the chagrin of a student who needs to prove that no matter how much he practices that passage, it won't improve.

"Pretend to be a beginning flute player and show us how breathy the tone would be," I suggested to a flutist wanting a clearer tone. As she concentrated on how to make her tone breathier, it kept edging over into clearness.

Over and over I find such things happening. A friendly skeptic asked what percent of the time such ploys do *not* work. It's a fair question, but I had trouble answering, for it seemed ridiculous to tell him how often they *do* work. And if one ploy does not work, there usually is another one that will.

But why? Why does the permission to be a bad sight-reader, to play the flute with a breathy tone, to play the scene like a melodrama, produce positive results when our over-conscientious efforts fail? It is an interesting paradox. Perhaps the sheer rebelliousness in giving ourselves permission to fail frees a childlike awareness and clarity. There is something in each of us that yearns for gentle, loving permission to make mistakes—to be a beloved child, loved no matter how much we goof. In that permission to fail is the embodiment, paradoxical as it seems, of our sense of worth. In it is that comforting reassurance that we are okay even when we make mistakes.

Cecily did not have to be a super-woman, super-voice student, and super-wife at the same time that she was finishing her degree. She could fail temporarily in some of her roles in order to achieve excellence in her academic work. When we give ourselves permission to fail, we at the same time give ourselves permission to excel. Some power seems to come roaring through that we hadn't suspected was there. There is a strong urge in each of us to use our capabilities; it is the potent urge towards living that we were born with. Yet many of us seem to have been indoctrinated all along the way with the propaganda that we were born with only lethargy and laziness and that we can only succeed by browbeating ourselves.

We try so hard to succeed, all of us. We try so hard to be good people, to avoid making mistakes, to live up to our own expectations, to live up to the expectations of our parents, friends, teachers. We practice so hard for our next lesson on the trumpet, the organ, the slide whistle, or the tightrope. We carefully prepare for the next performance, whether for the concert stage, for the executive conference, or for the more mundane scenes of everyday life.

We can't bear the mistakes we might make; we can't bear the censure and the criticism due us if we do poorly. What a tremendous amount of energy we invest in that effort to prove, over and over again, that we can succeed.

After all that trying, it is such a luxury to know that it is not only permissible to fail part of the time, but an essential ingredient of being human. And we find that the failing is not failing after all, but merely learning, if we can tune in to the information available in all our experiencing and not attach labels of *good/bad* or *success/failure* to experiences. Better yet, we sometimes find that when failure is permissible, success is also legitimate—yet not mandatory.

When my college pedagogy students did their laboratory teaching of piano to four seven-year-olds, they learned, with the children, to do *tinnikling*, a Philippine jumping dance/game using long bamboo poles. When the bamboo poles are tapped together lengthwise on the floor, you jump astride the sticks, and when the poles are separated you jump between them, in a variety of different rhythmic patterns. There was as much laughter from the college students as there was from the younger ones as they tried to coordinate their jumping with poles that never seemed to be in the right place. As we evaluated the session later, the college students were well aware of the obvious connection between learning tinnikling and learning rhythm. But more important, one of them commented on the pleasure of being in a situation where failing seemed to be as much fun as succeeding. That is a rare experience for most of us.

The word "fail," of course, ceases to apply if we know that whether we try something new or practice something old, we are merely gaining information. It's pretty hard to look for information when we dress up ahead of time in our black judge's robes and horn-rimmed spectacles. "Caught you, you miserable failure," is about all we can say in such garb. But when we take pencil and pad in hand and dress for a reporter's job, we can go for "Just the facts, ma'am. . . ." "Just clean, simple facts, if you don't mind, sir." No slanting or sitting in judgment or you're fired—on the spot. No editorials—leave that to the editor. We don't want your opinions, just straight reporting.

We hardly know how to play the new role. Those old labels of *success* and *failure* weigh so heavily in our briefcase that it's hard to keep them where they belong. One experience at a time. Easy now. Take that run again on the cello. Take that scattered-to-bits energy that was causing the tension, which in turn was causing the mistakes, and gather it together by sensing your mistakes on the octaves. Information. Feedback. Stop telling your hand what it ought to do. Find out what it *is* doing. Information. Find out how your elbow feels, where it is in space. Information. Find out what happens with your bow when the octaves are out of tune. Find out what your knees are doing to the cello. Information. And the mistakes begin to clear up. It is *not* magic. We are freeing our minds to be *aware* on a level that trying can't subvert, and judging can't undermine.

Gallwey describes "Self II" who is free to respond when we get "Self I," the judgmental self, out of the way. We can come up with many labels. Fritz Perls, in his Gestalt Therapy work, used the term "top-dog," An older term for the part of us that constantly monitors our existence is the "superego." The Society for Descriptive Psychology describes the "Overseer Personality" who criticizes us into immobility. In this book I talk about "inner judges."

The labels are unimportant. What is important is that we recognize our need for emancipation when the voices start their annoying buzzing in our ear—when they yammer at the edge of our consciousness. Too often the yammering has gone on for so long, so continuously, that our entire bodies are punchy with tension as we try to defend ourselves. Though we resent the way our inner judges beat us up, we are also convinced that we deserve the multiple beatings.

Check it out. Close your eyes and hear what some voice is telling you you should be doing right now rather than reading this book. "You should be practicing. . . . You should be taking the dog for a walk. . . . You should be writing long-neglected letters. . . . You should get at the monthly bills. . . . You should be clearing off your desk for the next project. . . . You should be studying for that exam. . . . You should relax. . . . You should be doing the dishes. . . . You should be resting. . . . You should go out for some exercise. . . . You should, should, should, *should,* SHOULD.

Our "shoulds" may never go away. But they can learn to keep their proper places in our lives, if we have the courage to talk back when they pile up into immobilizing forces that distract us from the task at hand. Cecily's "shoulds" were valid ones, yet they were crushing her until she confronted them. They dissolved into manageability when she shoved herself into her beekeeper's helmet and veil and laughed herself back out again. Her "shoulds" became wobbly when confronted by an impudent child. Anne's "should be sincere" admonition dissolved in the face of encouragement to be phony.

The next time you feel that familiar message inside your brain saying "should," pay attention. It may be a simple, straightforward message that you can deal with in simple, straightforward action. But if your "should" looks like Velcro, ready to snag you into guilt and over-trying and judging and groveling, listen with a new ear and be ready to talk back. Most of us can afford some impudence and humor in addressing these voices.

12.
Maybe
I
Like
My
Problems

"I never want to play this Brahms Rhapsody again, I'm so sick of it!" announced Valerie. Since she was committed to playing it in an up-coming audition, her sickness needed recognition, diagnosis, and treatment—not always an easy process.

I had a suspicion tiptoeing around in my head that she was tired, not of the piece, but of the problems. I asked her how she was practicing. Before she could answer, I said "Don't tell me; I already know," and described accurately what was happening. "You're playing the whole piece through from beginning to end, right? And you flinch and swear a bit each time you play in the cracks between the keys." I suspected that her judge would effectively beat her, and she would throw herself at the piece again, from beginning to end, with no new information about what was happening. I could almost see her dark eyes narrow, her jaw set and her body tense. *Next* time she would "do it right, stupid old piece." The more the music disintegrated, the more she would be convinced that it was just because she was so sick of the piece.

"How'd you know?" asked Valerie sheepishly. Then she added suspiciously, "Did you talk to my mom?"

How'd I know, indeed! No, I hadn't talked to her mom. I didn't need to.

Valerie was one of a group of junior high school students who worked together on a weekly basis. The group members shared my concern over her dilemma. Each of the other three could see what she was doing to herself and to the piece, and could also recognize an approach that was all too familiar in their own experience. Following my philosophy of group teaching, I turned the problem over to the group, knowing that as they helped her, they would be growing in their own awareness. They were loaded with ideas.

147

"Have you tried that opening with your eyes closed to see if you can sense the crossovers accurately?"

"How about analyzing? Remember how that opening theme gets transposed up a third, and how you don't hit a G minor chord until the fifth line?"

"How about the part you were going to practice in rhythms?"

"Oh come on, guys, I've tried *all* that stuff, but it doesn't really help."

That wasn't precisely true. She had effectively used similar ideas in the early stages of learning the piece, but at this stage she resisted that kind of effort. She wanted ready-made solutions or none at all. Mostly, she wanted to convince us that she was sick of the piece, that she couldn't play it decently, and that nothing—absolutely nothing— would help.

The most difficult stage in learning a piece is this stage at which we can play it well enough to impress our friends, but badly enough to convince ourselves that we will never get any better.

In the beginning, the process of learning is usually fun. We like the music, it is challenging, and the sounds are still new enough to be a delight each time we experience them. We are impressed with ourselves. It's like a new love affair. We can ignore our love's irritating habits because we are so caught up in the novelty of the relationship and because we have few expectations. It takes time to strip away the naivete of our vision, but inevitably the problems become apparent, and our love is tested.

The Mozart sonata that we read so easily becomes absolutely devilish in its demands for sparkling clarity. The position shifts in the viola piece increase in difficulty in direct proportion to our determination. The high C in the Mozart aria seems to keep getting higher and makes us lock our knees two lines before we sing it.

"I can't," we moan, so loudly that we convince ourselves.

The problems that were challenging when they were new develop a stale taste that dulls our appetite for practice. We invent excuses— indeed we don't even have to invent them, for who ever really has the time to practice? Or we conjure up a dose of self-martyring willpower and dive in. This is a nasty stage—the proverbial darkness before the dawn. And the dawn never comes if we get stuck in our problems and turn them into an addiction.

"Valerie, I almost get the feeling that you don't really *want* anything to help," someone ventured.

"Of *course* I want help. Don't be dumb."

"Do you *have* to play in the audition?" asked someone else.

Valerie looked at me, startled. "Absolutely not," I answered. "She has the option of competing at the state level since she placed at the district level. But she is under no obligation to play. In view of how she's feeling about the Brahms, she might just want to drop out and go on to new material." But I also knew that she needed the audition to help her through this stage of learning.

Faced with an option she hadn't really considered, Valerie knew immediately that she very much *wanted* to follow through and play in the audition. This meant, of course, that she might have to give up her addiction to her problems and her need to convince us of how insoluble they were.

Steve, one of the group members, sensed the change and pushed. "Hey, Valerie, remember how you felt when you first heard the Rhapsody?" She did.

"Okay, be two people—the performer and the listener—and pretend that you have never heard this piece before. Let the part of you that is the performer have fun impressing the listener. Maybe the listener will fall in love with it all over again." The actress in Valerie made a bow and took the cue.

The Rhapsody captured our attention as well as Valerie's afresh. We had grown as weary as she of the problems and of the piece, but by the time she finished there was no dearth of new ideas for carrying it further. Valerie no longer had any resistance to trying the suggestions, for she had made a choice—a choice on the side of solutions rather than problems.

"But only allow yourself *one* concentrated practice session with these new ideas and any others you dream up," I warned. "Then I want you to lay the Brahms aside and resist any temptation to play it for the rest of the week."

"How come? I'm all excited again and don't want to put it away."

I knew how easily the sickness could recur, and I knew Valerie well enough to know that if she were restricted for a week, working with the Brahms would become even more tantalizing. I also knew that some ideas had been planted that her subconscious mind would work with. Giving this process time to take place would make it easier to clean up the piece when she got back to it.

Her new enthusiasm held. The impossible became possible, and Valerie was almost flip about how easy the clean-up was. "Oh, the Brahms?" she responded a couple of weeks later, surprised we should ask. "It's fine. I love it! It's the Beethoven I need help with. I can't *stand* that piece any more."

So it goes!

The Brahms really *was* fine. Valerie had discovered for the first time in her life what can happen when we dare confront our addiction to problems. She will probably have to make that discovery a number of times before she is able to spot the early symptoms and deal with them completely on her own. But she now has a successful experience to rely on. She may first transfer that experience into the group by helping a peer through a similar period of disenchantment, accurately and quickly pinpointing that person's need to convince us of the insolubility of some problem.

Valerie learned many other things before she was through. She learned that in her audition nervousness she could forget to listen to what she was playing, and unknowingly ride the pedal on the unfamiliar piano, nearly ruining her by-now-beloved Brahms Rhapsody. She found that her fingers could run away from her brain in her Debussy piece. But she also found that she could get past her nervousness enough to show her audience the wondrously moving quality of a Beethoven sonata movement.

Success or failure? Neither. It is all feedback—information to be used. Before the audition we all spent considerable time exploring meaning in tricky words like "winning" and "losing." When Valerie was feeling really good about her pieces, her progress, and her growth in the last months, we had asked her if that growth could be either enhanced by winning or destroyed by losing. She thought a moment, then came up with the surprised realization that the results of the audition had little to do with *real* results—that nothing could alter her gains unless she allowed someone else's opinions about "winning" or "losing" to subvert her growth.

After these auditions Valerie had a new commitment to herself as she began working on new material, and she had a new clarity about sniffing out problems in the making. With each new learning adventure she will make further gains in problem-solving rather than in problem-creating, and little by little come to see the difference.

Often we assume that we can avoid problems if we are just more cautious along the way. "As you learn this new piece, remember how important it is to learn it accurately from the beginning," I remind a piano student. The conscientious student nods and practices cautiously. But there is a point at which caution is inappropriate, or else the musician will perform the piece as cautiously as he learned it. The cautious person will live out his life encumbered by galoshes and umbrellas, even on sunny days.

We can't practice our prize-winning dive in slow motion. It's top speed or nothing once we leave the diving board, and we learn by the humiliating pain of a belly-flop. I like the image of the time-worn phrase "fling caution to the winds."

When we take a leap, we take a risk. There are problems lurking. We may have learned a new piece carefully and meticulously. But meticulousness does not give meaning. When we have mastered the mechanics at slow speed, we push the tempo up one notch, then another. Still more. It should work. But suddenly the mechanics that worked at slow speed cease to be relevant. We have problems, try as we might to avoid them. Our problem-solving must reach a new level of sophistication.

"Linda, stop worrying about how often your fingers play in the cracks between the keys. Pretend you are an actress acting the part of a concert pianist, and the sound doesn't matter. It will be dubbed in later from a recording." Tim Gallwey uses a similar ploy on the tennis courts.

As Linda acted out the role, substituting authority for cautiousness, she startled us with a new sound. She forgot to worry about accuracy and power, and in a wonderful moment of drama they both came out of hiding to support her new role. She was ecstatic.

Barry was envious of the change, totally unaware that a similar experiment had caused an equally dramatic transformation in his own playing. "I must say you've made a believer of me by what just happened with Linda. But I still can't believe *my* playing yesterday was any different from the crummy mess it usually is." Sometimes we actually do change, yet still cling to an old image of ourselves.

We worked with him the following day and exchanged glances as changes again took place. This time he *couldn't* have missed it.

"Did it sound different to you that time?" someone asked.

"No. Why?" he responded, completely oblivious to what was happening.

We tried again. If it weren't for his obvious sincerity, we would have thought he was putting us on. Barry was aware of even subtle changes in other people's playing, and rejoiced for them. Yet he seemed happily dedicated to an image of his own mediocrity. Actually, Barry was a pianist with impressive ability, far from the mediocre image he held of himself. This image had developed a life of its own, separate from reality. His standard for his own playing was so high that he noticed only the difference between his playing and his high standard. He didn't notice even dramatic improvements in his own playing. But since he didn't have such unrealistic standards for the playing of others, he was free to notice their improvements.

"I have a problem." How often we accept this from someone not as a statement of fact, but as a challenge to our ingenuity to solve that person's self-proclaimed problem. We respond with over-zealous enthusiasm, always more eager to do battle with another person's difficulties than our own! Our perception is so clear, our intuition so unclouded—and our bafflement so great when the friend or student responds with something less than enthusiasm to our suggestions.

"I wish I could learn to hear what people are really saying when they ask for advice," wailed Barbara, a friend. Over and over she eagerly takes the bait when friends tell her their problems, without realizing how often all they want is a little sympathetic wallowing. Her good, practical, common sense advice to a friend on how to toilet-train a two-year-old had just been spurned, and she realized that once again she had obviously misunderstood an apparent plea for a solution. On reflecting, she could see the small drama that was being enacted in her friend's home, with the two-year-old and his toilet-training serving as a convenient arena for more important issues between her friend and his wife. The friend's need to complain outweighed his need for a solution to the problem. So although the friend really thought he was asking for help, Barbara, in her retrospective wisdom, could understand why he had reacted with such hostility when confronted with her perfectly sensible, obviously helpful suggestions.

Problems, unfortunately, can be addicting. Like it or not, we take a certain amount of pride in the very problems that distress us. Once we solve a problem, we find we have squeezed through the palings in the fence to face unfamiliar terrain. Next steps in growth may be exciting, but they may also be scary. If we are still caught in our struggle with a problem, the very familiarity of the struggle becomes reassuring, no matter how obnoxious it may seem.

We cry for answers and for advice. We spend huge amounts of money seeking help from teachers, doctors, counselors, therapists. Yet all too often we pack up our troubles in the same bag we brought them in and hug them to us. We may not like them, we think we want to dump them, but there is something pathetically human in the way we cling to them. "I thought *I* had problems. But I sure wouldn't want to trade places with Ralph." And Ralph shakes his head and looks at *me* and says, "I thought *I* had problems."

There seems to be a level at which we really do like our problems. After years of continuous pain from headaches, if I am confronted with the information that the pain stems from a mechanical dysfunction of my jaw that can be easily remedied, am I ready at all levels to part with my pain? "Of course," I say eagerly. "I am so sick of hurting. I am so very, very tired of constant pain. I have spent so many years trying to block it out. Please, I would do *anything* to be rid of that pain."

"But wait a minute," says a very small part within me that I refuse to acknowledge. "I'm not sure of my identity without the constant pain."

"Impossible!" I counter. The very notion is repugnant to me.

But that small, scared part has to be dealt with for the treatment to be totally effective; if not, the pain will either refuse to dislodge itself despite the effective cure, or it will conveniently jump to another part of my body.

"What is the cancer buying for you?" Dr. Carl Simonton asks patients in his cancer self-help program in Fort Worth, Texas. How could he be so unsympathetic and brutal to someone already suffering such trauma? He knows only too well that it is only the patient who can honestly face that question, who has a chance of ultimately answering with life instead of death.

"What does your problem buy for you?" I may have to search deep within me to answer that one. I'm not sure I have the courage. If I give up my addiction to this problem, what might be expected of me? Where might it lead? Am I ready to go on, or does it feel safer to muddle around in familiar puddles? The water looks deeper in the next one, even though it looks cleaner. And what about the puddle beyond that one? It's almost pond-sized. And what about the next—and the next?

"What does my problem do for me?" Try it out. It's safe enough to try a few answers. You can always back up if you become too fearful. No, I take that back. There is no backing up, for once you dare to answer the question you have already changed. You've opened the door a tiny crack to a sunbeam or two. So leave it alone if you're allergic to sunbeams.

"What does my problem buy for me?" Does my problem with performing insure a comfortable anonymity instead of a challenging career as a concert violinist? Or if I solved my problems with stage fright would I be free to choose with a wider view of my potential, a clearer sense of what brings me satisfaction and fulfillment? Am I honestly immobilized by my problems, or terrified by the possibility of success?

Do my headaches buy me respite from consuming demands from my family? Or could I protect myself intelligently and effectively without the headaches?

Do my problems with memorizing rescue me from the fear of performing? Or would solving those problems make performing into an option that might be pleasurable?

Does my problem with commitment buy me safety from disappointment in a relationship or a profession? Or would the growth—as well as the pain—of commitment be more challenging and interesting than the boredom of safety?

Close your eyes and play with the question, "What does my problem do for me?" Don't try to answer verbally. Just choose one problem. . . . Now get a clear image of yourself *without* the problem. . . . If the image isn't clear, if it's hard to imagine yourself without the problem, think of someone else who doesn't have your problem. . . . When you can see clearly how they function without the problem, imagine yourself as that person. Now step into that image and become yourself without the problem . . . functioning as you would wish . . . Follow yourself around . . . experience your joy . . . experience other people's reaction to you without the problem . . . Are they happy for you? . . . are they envious? . . . are they puzzled? . . . How do you feel without the problem? . . . are you at loose ends without it? . . . are you lonely for the problem? . . . Do you miss feeling sorry for yourself? . . . What protection did the problem give you? . . . What privileges or concessions might you have to give up without the problem? . . . What new expectations do you have to face now that your problem is gone? . . . Is success more frightening than problems? . . . Go back to your positive feelings about being rid of the problem, to your sense of release, of excitement, of anticipation . . . sense your added trust in your capabilities . . . make up an exaggerated scenario to dramatize your freedom. . . .

Go back and look at your problem, lying there in the corner where you left it. It's already collected a little dust. . . . Do you want it back? . . . Remember, even though you hated it, it did furnish you some protection. . . . Do you feel vulnerable without the familiarity of it? . . . Do you feel a little naked and exposed? . . . With this particular problem solved, do you perceive new problems? . . . Does the very solving of one problem open up new ones? . . .

Some of these questions are painful to answer. Problem-solving is complex business when we get past mere wishful thinking and misleading "if only's." "If only" emerges too often as a deceptive sigh which keeps us at a safe distance from success and from solving our problems. "If only" I had more time; "if only" I were more talented; "if only" I had more money; "if only" I had more support from friends or family; "if only" we were living in better times. "If only" pulls a grey curtain between us and the way things actually are and keeps us from seeing our way through to a stronger reality. It gives us a lovely excuse for puddle-muddling, either wishing for things that are impossible or refusing to move in the direction we think we want to move in.

The familiarity of our problems can be dangerously seductive. Although success beckons with one hand, it signals caution with the other. While we think we are responding to the hand that beckons, another part of us heeds only the caution. The part of us that holds back knows that change involves challenges—losses as well as gains. Change always means a little dying, a leaving behind of something old and tattered and no longer useful to us even though comfortably familiar.

If we like our problems too well, we need not risk the hazards of change. On the other hand, if we dare to leave the familiar tatters and inappropriate responses behind, we take our chances not only with the hazards of change, but with the challenges and excitement of success and growth. We stick our toes in fresh water that invites us to plunge, come what may.

13.
Clammy
Hands
and
Shaky
Knees

On the day of my first piano recital, I awakened with a stomach ache. It got worse as the day wore on, and by late afternoon my mother decided I probably shouldn't play that evening, but that I could go along to hear my two older sisters play. By 6:30 my stomach ache was lots better, but I didn't want to admit it. I dressed up in my new yellow dotted swiss dress and white pumps, looked in the mirror to see if I still looked pale enough to get by with not playing, and went with my family to the church where the recital was being held.

My teacher looked disappointed, but took my parents' word that I was well enough to come but too sick to play. "If you change your mind, just walk on up when it's your turn," she said matter-of-factly. I was glad she wasn't angry, but felt disappointed that she hadn't urged me on—at least a little. When I looked at my name on the neatly printed program, I almost told her I was fine. She was quite busy though, shooing the rest of the performers backstage to wait for the clock to tick its way to 7:30.

The church, rented for the evening, smelled of lilacs and starched dresses and old hymnals and spring breezes. As I sat down between my parents, I heard programs rustling behind us and the hum of voices as people chatted, and I suddenly knew people were reading my name on the program and wondering why I was sitting in the audience with my parents. They would think I wasn't ready! I scrunched lower to get away from the questioning eyes I felt from behind. Why couldn't we have sat in the back row? I leaned my head on my mother's shoulder and tried to look pale again, but instead my face got pink.

The magic hour arrived, the recital began. Piece by piece it marched towards my name. Only half of me listened; the other half of me mentally rehearsed what I would do when it was my turn to play: I'd urge my body to stand up, squeeze past my daddy's long legs, and scoot to the end of the pew. But then I would get stuck, my feet wanting to turn in two directions at the same time, either to take me up the carpeted steps onto the pulpit-stage, or out the big oak doors at the back of the church and a hundred miles away. My mental rehearsing came out in restless wiggles. My mother noticed, squeezed my hand, and whispered, "Do you want to play?" I shook my head, for though I did want desperately to play, I didn't want her to urge me. If I pried myself off that bench, it would have to be my own doing.

My stomach ache was back, and I didn't have to wonder why. I knew I was afraid to play; I also knew I couldn't bear *not* playing. I felt relieved, but I also felt cheated, sitting there in my brand new recital dress with red-hot piano pieces in my fingers. I wanted the audience to be clapping for me, for my pieces, for my curtsy which I had rehearsed so carefully.

Sally played next, just before my turn. Perhaps I could gather the courage to perform. One more time I rehearsed my long walk to the piano, and was still rehearsing when I realized people were already clapping for Sally. *Now . . . move, body . . . let me go on up . . . don't just sit here like a lump . . . move. . . .* My body balked. *Move, body—get up and start walking—*

"Eloise Stein is not feeling well tonight so we will go on to Damon Jones." *On no! I've lost my chance!* My face burned. *Another few seconds and I would have made it.* Made it? Made it where? I realized that the impetus to run was still as strong as the impetus to perform. That was why my feet wouldn't work. Now an entire year would have to trudge past before my feared and beloved Miss Cetti would schedule such a grand occasion again. My face got hotter as I felt a big sloppy tear quiver in the corner of my eye. I pretended my nose itched so I could rub it away, and stuffed the rest of the threatening flood back up into my bursting head. I made a vow about next time, also suspecting that my vow wouldn't keep me from getting scared again.

I didn't cop out the next time. But that first recital wasn't the last time I wanted to run away before a performance. It was not the last time I waged battle with feet that wanted to go two directions at once.

I remember what happened an hour before my first child was born. I had felt so ready, and so positive about the experience which I anticipated as the ultimate in fulfillment for any woman. A great performance was coming up, yet suddenly it terrified me, and I wanted to cancel the whole thing. *Just give me another day to get ready and get a little more used to the idea. Let me keep it in the future for just a little while longer, and I'll be magnificent!*

But I couldn't sit this one out on the bench and wait for next year's performance. This time I couldn't back out. Again I made a vow. I promised myself that once this small being whom I had loved so tenderly during my glowing pregnancy made it safely out of my drum-tight belly, I would never be tempted into a repeat performance. I'd stick to piano from here on.

Only a few hours later I could barely remember such a thought!

Giving birth . . . giving birth to a performance, to a book, a poem, a work of art . . . no—the poem, the book, works of art all belong in a different category. We don't concentrate the soul-searching into only a few intense moments. We spread the trauma out over a much longer period. It is in performance that the sudden panic hits, that we beg for release from our destiny and at the same time court the very experience that terrifies us. When the crucial moment to perform arrives, we try to talk ourselves into a calm state, and get even more tense. We try to convince ourselves that this much adrenalin is outrageous, but our knees only get shakier. We walk onstage and pretend the audience isn't there at all, but someone coughs and the game is up. A well-meaning friend says "There's nothing to get nervous about," and it almost helps, because the desire to strangle distracts us for the moment.

Once I had lived through the dramatic performance of giving birth to my child, my euphoria all but blotted out my previous fear. We can as easily forget the trauma that precedes a performance and pretend that we won't get scared the next time. But the next time catches up with us, and suddenly we're as scared as ever.

The fact that some fortunate people seem to bypass this kind of trauma seems hardly worth mentioning, for the rest of us can only stifle our envy. Such characters seem to thrive on performing—the larger the audience the better; the tougher the critics the more challenge. The few mild symptoms of nervousness they show ahead of time disappear the moment they walk onstage. It seems that their body chemistry works consistently *for,* instead of against them. As I said, we can only snuffle down our envy, assume they're bluffing, and face our own reality.

The reality we face is that once again we are dealing with inner judges who stand by ready to cut us down for the first semi-quaver that we drop. The English term "semi-quaver" for sixteenth note seems most appropriate here, for we certainly suffer enough quaverings and semi-quaverings! It takes but a moment of uncertainty and our judges are there as though we rang for them. Their yammering leaves us feeling as if our nerve endings have been rubbed with sandpaper. "You should have practiced more . . . you should have practiced better . . . the audience won't like you . . . what if you have a memory slip? . . . you're a fool to try this . . . they are expecting you to sound just as good as the last time . . . they are expecting you to sound better . . . you've got a weak spot on page three . . ." on and on. We toy with the idea of getting sick enough to cancel the performance, but we're grown up now and can't pull it off. Sometimes we settle for getting just sick enough to give ourselves an excuse if we don't do our best. I have a friend who now treats his attacks of bronchitis philosophically, for they arrive—always on schedule—just a few days before a big performance. In his mind, performing merges with fever and coughing and feeling miserable, and he has finally stopped trying to divert these attacks. He has enough to do dealing with his judges on the day of performance, so he accepts his illness with resignation.

Our judges are tricky and unpredictable. Sometimes they do their job early in the game and wear themselves out by the time of the actual performance. If we begin to count on this happening, they wait until the last minute and attack just when they have lulled us into thinking we have outwitted them. Or, worst of all, we walk onstage radiating confidence and play superbly, only to have our brain go fuzzy and our fingers develop the consistency of licorice sticks on the fourth page of the concerto. Devious judges sneak in at the precise moment that we allow ourselves a small pat on the back for how well things are going.

Perhaps the worst aspect of such experiences is that we feel like victims—victims of these judges, victims of some insidious process that takes over and leaves us powerless. Our bodies turn alien, ready to do us in. We have no sense of control—only a skidding sensation like hitting soft sand in a car going eighty miles an hour.

If, on the other hand, we happen to have a good experience without the usual overblown dramatics, in retrospect we try to assign significance to what we did or did not do the day of the performance. Let's see now—it must have been jogging five miles before breakfast, or eating half a pound of rare steak for lunch, or sleeping with lavender blossoms under our pillow, or finding a half-dollar in the subway. If we can just repeat the magic, we think we will have a reliable formula to use each time we perform, and we need never become a victim again. But the formula doesn't work the next time, because formulas have nothing to do with how our bodies respond.

Throw the formulas aside. They are worthless. Instead, play detective and go after some solid information about how your own body responds before and during a performance. Without the willingness to get that information, you could spend the next eighty years discussing stage fright and nervousness in theoretical terms and never make any progress.

Ready? Okay, here goes. In a workshop I might ask you "What are your symptoms?"

"I get really nervous before I play," you might say. "It gets so bad that I wonder if I should even perform."

"What do you mean by 'nervous'? I know what *I* mean by nervous, for my body has a code that spells out 'nervous' to me. But you will have to be more explicit for us to understand precisely what it means to you."

"I guess I mean scared."

"Not good enough. That's a state of mind. We want to know what goes on in your body."

"Well, when I get scared I get these nervous symptoms."

"Ah, now we're getting closer. What symptoms?"

"Let me think . . . they aren't always the same . . . oh, yes, my hands shake, and—" You laugh and add, "Ask me to perform, and I'll come up with a full set of symptoms."

That's precisely what I was leading up to. But first I wanted you to try to pin down what actually goes on in your body. Most people think they are giving an accurate description when they say they suffer from stage fright, or get nervous or scared, without realizing how many different sensations can carry the same label.

Next I might send you out in the hallway to work up a case of jitters before you play. "Don't come in until you feel nervous."

You spend longer in the hall than you thought you would, because now that I have ordered you to get nervous, you're having difficulty. You're feeling a little sheepish because you made quite a thing about this problem of yours. But you finally stir up a little queasiness and walk in. We applaud; you sit down at the piano and get ready to play.

"How are you feeling?" I interrupt as your hands get in position for the opening chord.

"A little scared, but not as much as usual, for some reason."

"Then get scared. We can't accomplish anything if you don't."

You try, and get even less scared. I wanted you to find this out. It's pretty important information. What ordinarily happens in other situations is that you try to *keep* from getting scared and end up getting *more* so.

"You're too relaxed. It will never do. Tighten your chest, pull in your shoulders and take little breaths in the top of your chest." It's not too hard to produce typical stage fright symptoms by mimicking some of the physical aspects. Stop reading for a moment and take the time to try it. The rest of the chapter will make more sense if you do. You can increase it even more by imagining an important performance and putting a few hostile, picky judges in your audience. So, tighten up, breathe shallowly, and get your imagination going. . . .

I ask everyone in the group to do the same thing and to wiggle a finger as soon as they feel something akin to stage fright. By the time you wiggle your finger you have lots of company.

"What's going on for you?" I ask. "I have a soggy feeling in my gut . . . my knees are shaking . . . hmm, and my mouth is really dry." Someone else has tight shoulders and feels close to tears. "How about you, over there by the window?" "My fingers are trembling, my heart is racing, and I feel the urge to run to the bathroom." Someone else contributes "Clammy hands. . . . My stomach feels like purple concrete. I feel really weak, and a little nauseated."

"Amazing. And you all thought you were talking about the same thing when you said you got nervous."

The list goes on. As we identify and share our physical reactions we feel less singled out by the gods for punishment. We usually decide that if we could choose, we would take our own dry mouth rather than someone else's nausea or grasshopper hands.

"Let's get back to that case of dry mouth you mentioned, and experiment while you are still feeling it. Close your eyes and concentrate on exactly how a dry mouth feels. As a matter of fact, see if you can make it drier. . . . Make it drier yet—as though it had been swabbed out with cotton, or blown dry by an air machine at the dentist's. . . . Run your tongue around behind the teeth to check the dryness. . . . Push the dryness to the point where it can go no further."

Take one of your own symptoms—clammy hands, shaky knees, or whatever—and apply the same principle of pushing it to the point where it can go no further. Do *not* try to control it or make it go away; try only to increase the intensity and see how far you can carry this particular symptom. . . .

Interesting, isn't it? If you are like most people, you will find you can't push your symptom past a certain point, and that when you reach that point the symptom actually reverses. Your saliva begins to flow naturally again, your knees stop shaking, your hands get respectably dry. You may find that almost as soon as you *try* to intensify a symptom, it begins to disappear.

The significance of this information impresses me each time I experience it again. It means we don't have to run scared every time some adrenalin hits us. We can stand our ground and ask for more, instead of gritting our teeth and trying to stuff all the junk back into the box. The more we try to stuff it all back in, the more it spills through the cracks and the more frightened we become.

At this point in a workshop, I would ask you to take your piece to the piano. I would welcome any signs of nervousness, for it gives us more to work with. I would, in fact, find every possible way to stimulate genuine nervousness to give you a chance to become thoroughly familiar with your own set of reactions. A little restless whispering, the sound of someone writing comments on a sheet of paper, the rustling of your score as someone watches it—these are always good for bringing your demons back. I'd rather you were never surprised by them again, because when you allow the surprise, you allow yourself to become a victim again. If you wear out the adrenalin over and over without suppressing it, you learn to take the adrenalin for granted. "Oh, that again," you shrug, and go about your business.

The most distressing symptom of stage fright I have ever encountered turned up in a large, half-day workshop. Stomach knots and dry mouths are at least not visible. Alice's affliction, however, was audible as well as visible. Adrenalin not only cued her hands to shake but also cued her nose to drip. The more she resisted, the more it dripped. Between the nose dripping, and the sniffing to suppress the drip, both Alice and her audience had an extraordinarily difficult time concentrating on the music. A dry mouth would have seemed a blessing in comparison.

I had not bargained for a drippy nose when I agreed to work with performance tensions. Although I commiserated with her, as did the rest of the group, I decided that this was a symptom I didn't feel easy about tackling. There were plenty of other problems I could focus on, so I could sidestep that one. I zeroed in on her shaking hands, for that was something I could deal with confidently.

The hands yielded rather easily, to her surprise, but in the middle of the second page she started sniffing and dripping. Still loathe to tackle that particular problem in such a limited time span with no chance for follow-up, I bypassed it again by asking what quality she wanted in that section of the piece. She was playing the last movement of Moussorgsky's "Pictures at an Exhibition," and wanted more breadth and power.

"Without trying for power, sense your solar plexus as you play." She had been trying to get power from her arms and shoulders rather than from a source deeper within her body. "Now sense the bones you sit on as they contact the piano bench." She settled deeper into her body. "Now sense the limitations of your power as you play." As she searched for limitations, the limitations began to vanish, and she became engrossed in surprising sensations of *increased* power.

We worked for several more minutes before someone noticed and smiled. Almost at the same moment, Alice noticed. "Hey, my nose. It stopped dripping! That's impossible!"

I was as startled and pleased as she. And I am still curious. Could I have tackled that symptom as directly as I had the others, and tried to intensify the dripping? I suspect I could have, embarrassing though it might have been. I will never know for sure. The roundabout solution proved interestingly effective, however, and managed to solve two problems at once.

This time I even tricked myself, for I really had not anticipated the outcome, and interpreted the results as partly luck. It was certainly a dramatic moment in the workshop, but I would not bet money on the possibility of repeating it. Could it be that I am still having trouble accepting the very principles I work with? Perhaps the element of luck was operating in that I had a subject who was willing to go along with the experiment with almost childlike openness. Had she been negative and resistant, she could easily have proved that her problems were insoluble. I say *easily*, then hesitate. I am not sure. If she had been negative, she would have been even more convinced of how easily she could intensify problems.

Perhaps once the problem of shaky hands yielded, her mind suggested subconsciously that the more difficult problem might also yield. The distraction provided by working with strength and power diverted her from trying to suppress her drips and sniffles and they disappeared on their own. That's my convenient theory, at least.

Alice wanted to try out the whole movement, so I sent her backstage to give the adrenalin a chance to hit again. I had only two requirements: that she keep her sense of curiosity about any sensations of nervousness she happened to feel, and that she not try to suppress anything she felt.

She walked onstage, took a bow, and proceeded with a remarkably drip-dry performance that was not dry at all in the sense of what she conveyed musically. Since she was free to be curious about symptoms and stop worrying about them, the energy that had gone into worrying now poured through her fingers. The follow-up on that particular problem with the drips was interesting. The problem simply disappeared, and has not returned in the past year and a half. I wish all our problems could evaporate so easily!

When I myself feel the effects of adrenalin before performing, I think that the knot in my stomach or my shaking fingers or the fogginess in my brain will get increasingly worse—that I am powerless and have no control—and that ultimately these symptoms will completely engulf and overwhelm me. When I confront the symptoms head-on and demand that they increase in severity, I challenge my body and discover that things can go only so far. My body can produce only so much adrenalin, and when I find out exactly how much and what it will do to me, I lose some of my irrational fear of it. I don't go over the precipice after all.

The initial step in confronting symptoms is the most difficult, partly because it is frightening, and partly because we are so used to battering away at our problems. Trying something new is scary, and we're scared to death already. When we find a secret door that slides open at our touch, we tend to dismiss it and go back to battering. Even though we hate it, it is at least familiar.

New ideas keep emerging out of my work with people who have stage fright problems. The clues that release them are different for each person, and impossible to predict in advance. One woman was nervous about performing a difficult new contemporary piece with the composer present. In a rehearsal beforehand, I encouraged her to try an improvised dialogue with me at the piano to release some of her tension. It took a while before she could trust her free, unplanned reactions to my unpredictable bursts of sound.

"Now, on your own, see if you can capture the quality—the essence—of your piece without trying to duplicate any of the actual sounds." She took the same energy she had experienced in our dialogue into her solo improvisation. When she carried the same sense of abandon into playing the piece, with no concern for right notes, the music spoke with a new sound. I caught a gleam in her eye when she realized that if she happened to land on a wrong note, she could pretend it was right and carry the mistake off with convincing flair. Of course she expected many more wrong notes than actually happened. She realized that her usual over-concern for accuracy had drained the spirit out of both her and the music. The spontaneity she had just discovered also gave her new insight into the nature of the piece itself. Turning loose like that at a concert still frightened her, however, and I had no idea when she left whether she would opt for caution or abandon in the actual performance.

Her newly-discovered dare-devil attitude won out at the concert, and left both her and the composer in smiles. She took the leap of enjoying the piece as though she were improvising it, and lost her fear. The piece, performed by another pianist, had been a failure at its debut in Carnegie Hall, so the composer was even more edgy than she about this second performance. Only after he told her how she had restored his confidence in his piece did she confess, "I had no idea if you would approve, but I decided to go for the excitement rather than worry so much about right notes." He assured her that he too would choose excitement over cautious accuracy any time, and also made a confession—he hadn't spotted any wrong notes. Wrong notes or no wrong notes, she had given him the gift every composer dreams of—a performance that went beyond his own conception of the piece. In the process, she demolished her own nervousness.

A high school violist came to me for several de-spooking sessions before an appearance with an orchestra. Performing did not terrify him as it does some people. He just felt generally ill-at-ease, selfconscious, and awkward in front of an audience. I tried to intensify some of his rather vague symptoms of nervousness, but since this approach seemed of no great value to him, I decided to try a new tack.

"Tim, pretend you're the greatest violist in the world. Show us how you would walk onstage and begin your piece," I said, knowing how playing a role can often spark more confidence. My husband happened to drop by the studio at that precise moment, and since Tim had blanched at my suggestion, I threw the challenge to Adam. Being a non-musician but a great ham, he had no trouble being a model for Tim. Tim and his accompanist doubled up laughing at Adam's portrayal of a concert artist who was supremely confident to the point of arrogance and who walked onstage with elegant deliberation, accepting his applause with a condescending nod. Tim and Adam created another character, taking turns until they were happy with their creation. Tim demonstrated by charging onstage with a confident stride and creating drama by the very way he lifted his viola into place beneath his chin. By the time his bow reached the strings of his viola—at the end of an exaggerated flourish—we were ready for the most gorgeous sound a viola could make. Tim lowered his viola and grinned.

"No, no, don't stop!" I said. "We've got to hear how this guy sounds!" Tim dramatized his entry again, even better than before, and this time launched into the beginning notes of his piece.

He startled us with sounds as dramatic as his act. Tim loved it, but felt he was cheating because he was play-acting. "Tim," I said, "when you play that convincingly, you aren't play-acting. How could you pretend to play a beautiful tone if you couldn't really produce it?" He shrugged, pleased with the possibility. "If I really believed I could play like that, I'd stop being nervous."

Right! But it took time and some exploration of other problems to convince him. He fretted a lot about staying with the orchestra, for instance. "That's not your responsibility," I told him. Let *them* worry about staying with *you*." That was a new thought. "I'll tell you what. Let's pretend you are conducting the orchestra with your own playing." The role of conductor encouraged him to take the initiative rather than worrying about following. When he played a more aggressive role, he began to look more confident. When he looked more confident, he began to sound more confident. When he sounded more confident, he gained more faith in himself, which took him full circle back to looking more confident. He had started out with a little-boy stance, with his feet too close together and locked into place, giving his body a narrow insecure base. With each experiment, his stance widened and gave him a more secure base with freer, more fluid movement in his body. The image of a mature, seasoned performer began to emerge.

Over a period of several weeks Tim began to claim the new image and the sound that went with it. He stopped worrying about whether it was phony or not, and the phoniness disappeared. Backstage after his performance, he accepted compliments about his stage presence and poise with almost unnerving sincerity. He had left the uncomfortable little-boy feelings behind so many days ago!

The more I work with performers, the more I realize how enormously complex and varied their problems are. Some performers gain from learning techniques of relaxation, self-hypnosis, autogenic training, or biofeedback. I've tried something related to biofeedback by having students use some tiny little 15¢ thermometers that I bought in a college bookstore. Each student lies on the floor or sits comfortably, holding a thermometer between a thumb and finger. (Biofeedback finger tapes that register temperature are great, but fairly expensive.) After checking initial temperature, I talk students through five minutes or so of sensing warmth in their fingers, feeling their arms get warm and heavy, and pretending they are lying on warm sand at the beach or warming their hands at a campfire. When we stop, they re-check their temperatures and find they have gone up several degrees—for some even as much as ten or more. I have tried something similar, but without thermometers, in large workshops by having people simply concentrate on one finger without consciously trying to raise the temperature. As they stare at a finger, they soon begin to feel a tingling and warmth.

If we know we can control finger temperature, we have one more bit of evidence that our bodies are responsive and changeable. The same type of exercise can be used to change other body sensations such as tension. You can just register on a mental scale from 0 to 10 the amount of tension you feel. If you can stay detached, the tension usually drops.

People come up with dozens of questions relating to problems of stage fright, nervousness, and tension. There are no easy, pat answers to any of them. For instance, what do you do if you're in the middle of a performance, and just as you congratulate yourself on how well things are going, you begin to do poorly? The orchestra is a quarter of a beat ahead and you panic, even though you know the music inside out and upside down, and felt superbly confident until a split second ago. To recover from this kind of situation, you need to do more than just try to increase your stage fright. The solution needs to be much broader.

You already know that if you take further time to berate yourself and try to force your fingers to catch up, you may never make it. Instead, find something specific to pay attention to that might be useful. *Measure* the gap between you and the orchestra rather than fight it, and chances are the gap will close. Find the pulse of the orchestra in your own center, and your fingers will have a hard time resisting playing to the beat of that pulse. If your fingers fumble from panic, get into them. Inhabit them with your whole being. Put eyes in them, ears in them, and sensing devices that detect the temperature of the keys and the texture of the ivories. Sense the soles of your feet, the middle of your back, your rib cage, your elbows.

How can any of this help? It takes you out of your head and puts you into your body. It makes a connection between you and something real—something you can see, hear, or feel. It rescues you from vague internal rumblings that distract you from your playing. It momentarily tricks you out of the left-brain area of your head which is playing judge and dictator again, and activates the right-brain area which knows it knows the piece and doesn't waste time giving commands and making recriminations.

Such connecting relates to far more than the panic of the moment. If we respond only to that panic we begin dreaming up band-aid patches and slings (like practicing a measure 100 times in a row) that sound like cures, but that in reality separate us from our deeper needs.

As I work with the interrelated, yet varied problems of stage fright, I often bypass seemingly obvious remedies. For instance, I rarely tell anyone simply to relax, even though the tension is obvious, and though I urge people to explore relaxation techniques on their own. Have you ever tried to relax when you are doing your best to hang on to the disappearing theme of a Bach fugue? "Relax what?" scream your fingers as you try to figure out what and where and how much.

Tense muscles caught in the act and reprimanded are like children caught in the act of being naughty. "Stop being tense" is as hard to obey as the command to a crying child "Stop your crying or I'll give you something to cry about." Recognition of why the child is crying is a better approach. "You must feel really sad," said to a child makes the crying so legitimate that the crying usually ends sooner. In the same way, recognition of tension supports not the tension, but rather the body/mind team which has a way of dealing with tension on subtle levels. Actually, we don't want to get rid of all the tension anyway, so the word *relax* is inaccurate. We only want to get rid of the *extra* tension that does all the damage.

If you want to experiment with that, do an instant freeze as you sit reading this book, and check for excess tension over and above what it actually takes to hold the book. . . . Get up and walk around the room. Hold it. Before you even got out of your chair, did you detect extra effort? . . . Experiment with standing in front of the sink doing dishes. Does it take that much effort to swish warm suds around the smooth contours of a saucer? How about lifting a plate to transfer it to the dishwasher—was that shoulder clutch really necessary? . . . Take a sheet of paper and a pen and start a letter, or copy something. Are you holding that pen as if it might escape if you don't get a powerful grip on it? Do you think that the ink won't flow unless you force it out by clenching your jaw, or making your tongue or elbow tense?

It's not hard to get the picture. If we are this over-zealous in simple tasks, it's little wonder we mess ourselves up when we perform. Now go back to the way you hold the book as you read. Don't consciously try to rid yourself of extra tension. In fact, try your best to hang on to unnecessary tightness.

When I try this myself, I find it takes effort to hang on to tension. My body instinctively wants to let go the instant I recognize the tension. Each time I repeat the exercise, I lose a little more tension.

If I trick myself into relaxing my attitude, I have a head start on the problem. This explains why permitting, accepting, and even intensifying whatever is going on, accomplishes more than we might suspect. All these indirect techniques *do* have a reason for working!

Permission. The very word relaxes a spot in my center and lets me take a deep breath. If I can permit myself to feel scared, I can also permit myself to reinterpret the scared feelings as excitement, for excitement and fear come from the same adrenalin. I can even welcome the rush from the adrenalin and know that without it my performance would be a little too relaxed and bland, a little too predictable. When I allow the adrenalin to surge, I use the energy it provides instead of fighting it. I live a little dangerously, and you in the audience pick up the excitement and bounce it right back to me. The moments when I have felt that interchange between myself and an audience have been special, and they did not come about because I managed to put a lid on my nervousness, but because I used it.

Sometimes in a workshop, after a vigorous warm-up that leaves people out of breath with hearts racing, I ask them to describe the sensations in their bodies. They usually interpret these feelings as positive, stimulating, and energizing. Then I ask them to imagine a performing situation and see if they find any similar physical reactions. They often find the same heart-thumping, pulse-racing sensations and realize that in one case their reactions felt like "excitement," and in the other case they labeled the same symptoms "nervousness."

A university student wrote me a note after her senior piano recital, saying "In the pre-concert rush of my pulse, I was reminded of our session. The physical symptoms *are* the same as after a stimulating warm-up, and this time I was able to lean into them."

This recital had terrified her, for she had gone back to music school when her children were half-grown, and she had never given a full recital in her life. When she had performed previously, she felt little joy. She said she had felt trapped and closed in, as though she were in a dark narrow tunnel, and telling herself to relax had not helped. This time, when she remembered to reinterpret the fear symptoms, she felt a very different, positive sense of wanting people to hear her, and had the interesting sensation "of my energy splashing outwards towards the audience." She also remembered to breathe into the middle of her fear, which gave her a chance to collect the energy that had gone into that fear and use it in the performance, instead of using more energy to fight it.

Over and over I find that stage fright needs to be confronted and experienced in order to be conquered, and that each time we tell ourselves "Just control yourself," or "You'll be fine if you just forget about it," we either get more nervous, or we drive the nervousness underground only to have it sabotage us later. Each time we take it on we gain more courage. Each time we experience even modest success, we build a little more faith into our bodies.

I have gone in many different directions in this chapter, and there are many more still to go. You will find clues to some of your problems here; you will find even more as you start experimenting on your own. Some of what you read here may work immediately for you; some of it won't do a thing for you; some of it will work in time. And let's face it: there are times when nothing seems to work, and times when we are not psychologically ready for the success we think we want.

While we're at it, let's face something else. Part of the time when nothing works, we deserve to have nothing work because we are trying to coast on incomplete slap-dash preparation. If that's the case, no amount of hocus-pocus at the performance itself will have much effect.

If your behind-the-scenes preparation is secure, however, you deserve to have it work. You deserve to claim success. If you are willing to explore in some new directions, you need not continue to be a victim of your adrenal glands.

14.
"So You Were a Flop!"

That's what he said. Straight out. To Judy, my tender sweet ten-year-old. My Pakistani friend, Moin, just looked at Judy after he heard the story of what had happened at the recital. The piano had suddenly looked so foreign to her that she couldn't find the right starting note for her piece, and she had miserably blundered her way through her performance. Without any regard for how hard I had worked to make her feel okay about it, he blurted out, "So you were a flop!"

I was outraged. This is the kind of insensitivity that can damage a kid for life. *Blunt, rude, callous*! I fumed to myself.

Judy did a startled double-take, then to my astonishment let out a giggle. Moin grinned and put his arm around her and she giggled some more. Then she cried a bit and laughed some more and told Moin how dreadful it had been, and ran to the piano to show him how her piece really should have sounded.

Her agony dissolved, all because Moin was honest enough to label a flop a flop. It was years ago, and I can't remember what I had said to Judy. I know that I tried hard to let her know it was okay, I still loved her, I knew how she must have felt, it wasn't as bad as she thought (It was *just* as bad as she thought), everybody understood, etcetera. All my reassurance had only made her silence more silent. I could feel the way her skin seemed to push everything together into one solid mass inside her body.

So Moin said out loud to her that she was a flop. What a relief! Suddenly she knew all the stuff I'd been trying to tell her but that she had barely heard. *Of course I'm okay. Of course they still love me. And yes, it was just as bad as I thought. It was so bad, in fact, that it's even a little bit funny. And who cares if anyone understood—wouldn't it be a riot if they thought I always play Mozart that way? Just wait until next time. Just because that stupid piano didn't have a cracked ivory on middle C like ours at home, it threw me off.*

Both Judy and I learned much from the ordeal that afternoon because the five words "So you were a flop" were said without judgment. The simplicity of the statement carried with it the obvious assurance that Judy *herself* was not a flop—that she could fail many times and she would still not be a flop.

We have all had many experiences of failing and falling grandly on our rumps at embarrassing moments. Recovering from such a fall is not something we are prepared for. How difficult it is to say it to myself: "So you were a flop." Yet how therapeutic it is when I can manage to pull it off. I become my own friend, for it takes a tremendous amount of energy to pretend something went well when it didn't.

If I can approach a performance ahead of time with the question "So what if it's a flop?" do I set myself up for failure? Or do I give myself the privilege of being whatever I happen to be at that moment, without condemning myself ahead of time? The paradox is, of course, that when we are free enough to allow a flop, we are usually free enough not to have one. We can thumb our noses at our judges and say "So what?" They can huff and puff at us without effect, and we can go about putting our energies into the performance.

Our minds are tricky and complex and full of surprises. I'm a great advocate of approaching life with a strong positive attitude, but a positive attitude by itself never produced a fine performer. There is a whole choreography leading to that fine performance, and it involves a lot of plain old hard work. Somewhere along with the hard work must be the permission to blow it. With that permission, we can afford to be a little more reckless in what we dare. As we become more reckless, we also become more committed, for we know we are stretching ourselves.

Think of the times in your life when you have dared the most. Were those the times you blew it? Or were you more apt to crash when you were overly cautious with your talents? When we withhold the fullness of our capabilities, we diminish those capabilities. When we explore beyond where we feel safe and secure, we discover abilities beyond our expectations.

Hoarding begets shrinking, while daring begets expansion and opening up new corners in our consciousness. Each time we open up a new corner, we discover more corners we hadn't known about. Frustrating perhaps, but it gives life a fine excitement.

I have had a recurring dream for years. I am in a house that seems totally familiar. The dream has endless variations, but always at some point I discover a room or rooms in the house that I hadn't known about, or I realize that I knew about the rooms at one time but had forgotten they existed. The dream is always suffused with my delight in discovering new rooms, and I immediately start making plans for putting the rooms to use.

The dream first appeared when I had a desperate need to discover forgotten "rooms" within myself. Without such a supportive and prophetic dream, it might have taken far longer to explore the house that is me. At times I reject the dream momentarily when I feel I have too many rooms in use already. Yet it always alerts me to an unrecognized need to stretch in yet another way.

We can never close off our consciousness to these new airy spaces that need inhabiting. If we try to seal them off, a breeze comes through the cracks and creates an annoying draft. We do better to confront these new spaces and find what they have to offer.

If you are a performer, such exploring may lead to fresh new ways of exploring your field, turning your old ways inside out and upside down and risking a few flops along the way. It can mean dissecting your practicing and discovering why some of it feels like grating woody carrots on a dull grater. Mentally check a typical practice session with a curious eye. What part of it is productive and satisfying? What part of it is boring, or frustrating, or ineffective? There will be some of all these qualities, but often we get stuck with too many of the negative ones. We get stuck with *making* ourselves learn, forcing the new repertoire into our brains, rather than finding out how a particular piece can become part of us.

I have a tendency to put unreal demands on myself when I start a new piece. Lately I have wanted to show myself how effective all my new techniques are. So I push to get a new piece learned in record time just to prove something. Invariably I get in trouble unless I catch myself in the act and re-evaluate what I am doing. What I usually discover when I feel the familiar push is that I'm not using my new discoveries nearly as much as I am using old outworn habits. My husband, a non-musician though a music appreciator, helps me occasionally when I get myself in a fix. "How would you help someone else solve that problem?" he asks. My impulse is to stick my tongue out at him and send him back to his study, even though it was I who dragged him out to listen to a newly-learned piece. But I'm usually grateful at some level for the reminder, and I don't pout for long. When I investigate what has been happening, I am appalled at how much old garbage I have allowed to sneak back in. Often I have "programmed in" an excess of muscular tension in the difficult parts that guarantees clutching in the measure ahead. Or I have pretended that my mistakes are accidents. Or I have polished out the exuberance.

Whatever it is, it's time to pull it all apart and find out what is going on. It's time to re-read this book and learn again what I forgot I knew. It's time to humble myself by playing for students and inviting their comments. (Why did I train them to be so perceptive?) It's time for a massage session on old outdated muscle knots invited back by my folly.

Old junk, old habits, old knots. When can I be rid of them once and for all! When can I say "Aha, I've found that consistent state of awareness that lets me be—that leaves me free for unfettered learning." When will I arrive at the point when I can have a clean learning experience from beginning to end—with a piece of music or in life—without subterfuge from hidden layers within myself?

It is not to be. I need not waste time in wishing. It is enough to whirl around in the middle of my Prokofieff sonata and chase my judges out of sight when I catch them hanging over my shoulder. I am not a concert artist. I am a teacher and a writer, and I love to perform from time to time. I am at this stage of understanding and at this level of performance and with this much technique at my command. By the end of the day, or the week, or month, or year, I will be different—at a different level of performance, with a different level of technique at my command. Always I can go from here to there—or backslide from there to here during the times when I can't practice. And that's all right too, even though I may be frustrated. During the time my fingers can't get near a keyboard, other parts of me grow and give me more to come back to the piano with.

Shortly after I started writing this book, the local music teachers' association bought a new piano and planned a dedication concert. When they asked for volunteers for the concert I blithely signed up. I can always afford to be optimistic a few months in advance.

As the date approached, I knew it would only be sensible to cancel my performance, for my writing schedule on top of a busy teaching schedule on top of family needs made it unrealistic to hope for adequate practice time. But I had a stubborn streak that hung on and refused to let me make the necessary call. The performer in me was crying for some attention, and I was hungry to try out for myself some of the new insights I had gained in working successfully with other performers. At times I was envious when I helped others prepare for a performance. I realize how the work we do with others often reflects our own needs and desires.

I plunged wholeheartedly into what limited practice time I could find, and took great delight in discovering how my fingers and my psyche responded to new understanding. All went well as long as I still had a comfortable margin of time. I was able to use my time at the piano in a way that had never been possible before. There were ups and downs when I had to yank myself out of the old habits and nudge my brain anew, but the process was stimulating and gave me confidence. Then a few weeks before the concert, I cracked my tailbone in a skiing accident. Sitting at a piano bench was excruciating—in fact, impossible—for a time. By the time I could bear it, I was scared, for I had very little time.

The inevitable happened. I did everything I write about *not* doing. I listened to every judge in my private gallery—*you're out of practice, time is running out, what if your mind goes blank?, your reputation is at stake, that run in the Chopin might fall apart, yak, yak, yak.* I responded in classic fashion: *work harder, work longer, work later each night, push, push, knock yourself out, you've got to prove you can do it, it would be chicken to back out, it doesn't matter how tired you are, just conjure up some more will power, force your body a little harder.* This went on with my consent and knowledge at one level, yet at another level I denied what I was doing. Three nights before the concert I asked a friend who was rooming with us at the time to listen to me play. It was the end of a heavy day of teaching and I was clutching at the time I could finally claim for myself. I was clutching at more than the time—as though I could force that time to yield security and confidence and superhuman technical facility.

I tried to summon up enthusiasm I was too tired to have. I conjured up strength I didn't feel, and prodded my body through the piece. Julie made no immediate comment on the performance. What she did comment on was the obvious fact that I looked like I needed a soak in a hot tub. "You know, Eloise, I've been hearing these pieces a lot for the last couple of weeks. What are you worried about? You've been sounding great. But I don't like what you've been doing to your body the last few days. And tonight you look really ragged."

All too true. I wilted, feeling fatigue clawing at my bones. But she didn't understand. Sure, a hot tub would be great. Of course I would like to relax. But I had a full schedule the following day, and there were spots in the Chopin Impromptu that were falling apart, and even though the George Crumb piece was going well, who could tell what would happen Sunday? I was also doing an improvisation with a trumpet player and though we had improvised many times together, we had not done so recently and how did I know it was *really* going to work in front of an audience? I went to bed irritated because Julie didn't understand how impossible it was for me to let up at this point.

The next morning I wakened with headache trolls hammering away inside my head. I lay there feeling angry and frustrated. It was all too clear what I had been doing to myself. *Great job*, I told myself. *You can help other people through their problems, but when it comes to yourself, you blow it. You've really done a job. Talk about judges— you've made advance reservations for several dozen. And you're the one who's writing a book about this kind of stuff? Physician, heal thyself*, I thought wryly.

But what's this, floating through all the rest of my thoughts? Echoing so faintly that I pretended not to hear was Moin's voice from years ago. "So you're a flop. So you're a flop. So you're a flop!" Insistent, that voice. What's it saying? And with a reassuring grin? *"So you're a flop." Me? A flop? Me? Hey, you're right*! And wonder of wonders, it was somehow okay when I said it out loud. I could still love myself. I chuckled out loud in relief, and some of the headache trolls skittered off. What a marvelous phony, able to act out the reverse of everything I believed in, everything I taught, everything I wrote about. Up to this point, a flop.

Then I thought about Sunday's performance coming up, and the trolls sneaked back with their hammers. This business was not finished. I had flunked Act One and I could live with it, even laugh about it. But Act Two was coming up and I wanted to do well on stage.

I lay there listening to a small battle within myself. One part of me still said *Come on, you've got to make up for lost time and practice extra hard today or you'll never pull it off on Sunday, no matter what*. But that remark of Julie's about a hot tub kept bouncing around in between the hammer blows. By the time I dragged myself out of bed, I knew I needed a different script for my day. I made a few phone calls and realized how ridiculously easy it is—when we make a decision—to cancel our busy-ness.

I made one more phone call to the hot tub spa and then asked my husband if he wanted to go along with me. "Go along where?" he asked suspiciously. "A hot tub? In the middle of the day?" He thought I was being funny, but was so startled when he realized I was serious that he startled me by canceling his equally busy day. We looked at each other through the bubbles in the steaming tub and giggled like a couple of kids playing hooky. I felt the first layer of knots begin to melt, but wasn't about to settle for one layer. "Do you really feel okay about not practicing today?" my husband asked, getting nervous that maybe I was carrying this too far. I yawned and purred and stretched. "Mmmm." He asked me half an hour later, and I just wiggled a toe as I watched it float up to the surface. He decided I was hopeless so he wiggled a toe back at me.

On the way home from the hot tub spa, I stopped by a pianist friend's house. My friend knew I was feeling apprehensive about the performance and asked me if I would like to run through my pieces. I was still rubbery from hot-tubbing, but decided I would give it a go. My playing surprised me.

"What are you stewing about?" asked my friend, sounding a little irritated that I had made such a fuss when we talked the day before. "And by the way, what have you been doing technically lately? I'm impressed." So was I, as a matter of fact. Hmm.

I enjoyed avoiding the piano for the rest of the day except for half an hour or so of slow, thoughtful, relaxed work. Each time I felt a wave of nervousness, I countered it with advice straight out of my book: *Pay attention to how it feels. Track down the physical sensations. See if you can intensify what you are feeling.* I found out again first-hand that when I command my nervousness to increase, it balks and sneaks away.

I also fantasized what would actually happen if I blew the performance. The projected consequences were surprisingly dull. They had nothing of the dramatic flavor that had crept into my judges' scenario earlier. I had the image of some people being sympathetic and understanding (how I hate sympathy at such a time), some people being sharply critical, some people being glad because my failure made it legitimate for them to fail at times, and some people not paying much attention. Not much was really going to change in the world around me, either way. Astonishing! As another friend said to express what she felt in the middle of a performance, "I knew that the bus that went roaring past as I played was the same bus I would be on tomorrow and the next day and it didn't really make a great deal of difference what happened today." For her, also, that realization was freeing, and in no way encouraged lackadaisical nonchalance in her playing.

As I played around with the possibility of failing and once more being a flop, my world did a flip. Once I felt it was okay to fail, I was no longer afraid of doing so. If I did flop, for whatever reason, well then, okay, but I knew I didn't need to. I knew the music inside out and upside down and could trust that knowledge. I could trust the work I had done, for it had been good work despite the time problems and a cracked tailbone and some unnecessary self-punishment. I could trust my memory, for I had given it trustworthy input. I had confidence that I could handle any problems that turned up in the performance. My negative images of judges and criticisms dissolved, as had the knots in my muscles in the hot tub. I was free to play as well as I was prepared to play without worrying about "what-ifs." I was free to concentrate now on a positive image of myself playing well, for once I have permission to fail, I must give my imagination the strongest possible image of success. Oddly enough, the *permission to fail* and the *image of success* are not contradictory. It is the *fear* of failing, the terror that lurks in dark corners, that tugs us apart.

As it turned out, I played a little better than I was prepared to play—an interesting phenomenon that sometimes happens when we allow the adrenalin to spice things up. I also played a little worse than I was prepared to play, for I left out a line of the Chopin and lost a stray note here and there. But the charge was there, the excitement of putting a picture in a frame by feeling the responsiveness of my audience, by feeling something surge through the music that can never surge in quite the same way when I play to the four walls of my studio. This is what performance is all about, I realized, despite all the agony I had gone through.

I thought about it a lot afterwards. Nice ending, this time. *What about the next time? Will you get yourself into the same kind of jam?* Possibly. But maybe I can stay friends with myself long enough to keep my sense of perspective. Maybe I can chuckle my tensions away earlier in the game, before I go through so much pain.

Then again, maybe I'll forget all I know and hit a snag and really blow it. If I do, I hope a friend will be there to give me a hug, look me straight in the eye and say, "So you were a flop!"

15.
"Who Me? Did I Play That?"

Dump trucks, graders, "cats" with fiendish back-up beeps, jack-hammers—everything imaginable to help in widening and beauti-fying our traffic-marred, chuck-holed street—arrived one summer morning. Unfortunately I had just started the opening session of an improvisation workshop for a group of pianists and instrumentalists. The heavy equipment roared into action right in the middle of a period of silent imagery in which people were exploring their private worlds of fantasy and imagination.

Although I tried to block out the disruptive snarls and beeps and clangs, I repeatedly found my attention drawn to the obnoxious sounds. Finally I stopped trying, and in the same moment found the sounds sneaking into my consciousness as a symphony of contempor-ary sound, complete with driving rhythms, surging crescendos of sound, and dramatic contrasts in timbre.

"Keep your eyes closed," I told the group, "but forget the imagery and just pay attention to the sounds outside. Find out what you hear when you really listen."

It was a moment of revelation. We found ourselves listening for several minutes to the impromptu improvisation outside the window, fascinated with the changes in our perceptions. One moment we were jangling with frustration, the next we were listening eagerly for new developments in our symphony. One moment we heard nothing but noise, the next we heard music. During momentary lulls, the sound of a child's laughter and the delicate trill of a house finch gave us exquisite pleasure in contrast to the heavy brasses and percussion of the street crew.

"What a great introduction to improvisation! How did you ever arrange it?" asked someone. "I never stopped to think that we're almost constantly surrounded by improvisations of all kinds, yet we usually spend a lot of energy tuning them out."

"How about improvisation in movement?" I asked. "Did you each rehearse coming into this room this morning or did you improvise it?"

As we talked, we realized that we actually improvise everything we do, from the way we walk down the street to the way we prepare a meal. Can you imagine speaking without improvising? What if we used language as a rehearsed act, with memorized pieces like greeting cards for all occasions? Yet the word *improvisation* terrifies most people, musician and non-musician alike. The very thought conjures up images of being exposed and vulnerable. Whenever people break through these barriers of their own selfconsciousness, however, they find a wistful kid waiting for permission to be natural and free, and to thumb a nose at the polite predictability of everyday life. Recognizing improvisation in what we normally do gives us opportunity to infuse life with the sparks and flickers that we ordinarily subdue.

"Let's try another experiment," I suggested. "As we talk, pay attention to each gesture you make, each subtle move of your body, each shift of position, each word you choose to use in speaking—not in a self-critical way, but with a soft, relaxed sense of interest." We launched into a discussion of why each person had chosen to take this particular class. It was an easy subject, and allowed people to observe themselves gently as they participated.

"I never would have guessed how much goes on in my body as I talk," said one woman whose whole body dances when she talks. Some found more subtle responses, but each person had a sense of the spontaneous choreography taking place, both individually and as a group. We realized that although we each have a vocabulary of certain characteristic movements, these familiar movements weave themselves into new patterns in each new situation in our lives.

I divided the group in half, and asked one group to explore movement in a way that was totally random, with no response to movements of other people in the group. It was an impossible assignment. Try as they might, they could not keep their individual movements separate and isolated. As we watched, the supposedly random movements arranged themselves into interconnected patterns, as had the sounds outside my window. In fact, we realized that not only were the movements interconnected within the room, but that they also related to the sounds still invading the room.

We carried the experiment further with two people attempting a dialogue of unrelated sounds on bongo drums. Again, it was impossible. This experience led directly to the same sort of lively, animated interchange—using the rhythm of speech—that I usually use as a warm-up for improvisation. The bongo drums passed around the group until everyone had a chance at a dialogue with someone else. There was no longer any pretense at making random sounds as they discovered how many ways they could communicate on drums. They found they could shout, plead, explode in angry protest, back off and be infuriatingly passive. They could express anything from joy to moroseness, from tenderness to fury.

Drums connect us with emotions which we ordinarily suppress but which feel safe when they erupt spontaneously in drum talk. I drummed steadily with a friend for over an hour once, and felt temporarily purged of every frustration in my life. My friend promptly went out to buy a big Conga drum like mine, for he had felt the same release. Drumming in a group, freely embroidering a basic pulse, sends rhythmic pulsations through our entire bodies. If you don't have drums handy, sit cross-legged facing a partner and use each other's bodies as instruments, slapping knees, shoulders, arms, heads (gently!) in a free-wheeling dialogue. Upend a wastebasket and beat on it. Beat on the floor, clap your hands, get to your feet and dance your heart out, or tap out a rhythm on a convenient back. The scene livens up in any group when the juices start flowing and we begin connecting with real feelings. Interesting improvisation doesn't grow out of subdued politeness, but out of the energy of authentic emotions.

This group sounded authentic enough to move on. Earlier a number of the people had expressed discomfort at the thought of improvising at the piano or whatever other instrument they played. They felt they had invested so many years in their skill that it would be difficult to abandon their attachment to written music and right notes. I had assured them that when we enter the world of free improvisation, right and wrong notes cease to exist. I also knew they each needed to find this out on their own. This had to be a self-discovery for each person.

As we shoved the drums aside, I could feel people tense up as the moment of truth arrived. It had not been hard to coax them into uninhibited playfulness with the bongo drums because there wasn't a professional bongo drummer in the bunch to pass judgment on anyone. What emerged on drums had proved exciting and full of impromptu contrasts. But now their shyness crept back as they anticipated approaching their own instrument.

"Keep the same partners as when you were drumming, and go to the piano like a couple of kids pretending to be concert pianists. Pretend you've never had a piano lesson in your life."

I could feel their bongo-drum innocence returning. There is something about a keyboard with its intriguing pattern of white and black keys that tickles untrained fingers with an urge to explore.

"Keep the sense of dialogue that you had on the drums. You can respond to each other with a single word or a long sentence. Be impudent, angry, or whatever. You can even be rude and interrupt each other. Invade each other's territory on the keyboard and get as wild as you want."

The flutist and the cellist in the group volunteered first, for they could claim the same innocence at the piano as the rest of us on drums. They kept the same spirit of adventure at the piano. Another pair, both of them pianists, had difficulty initially because their fingers automatically sought out familiar chords and patterns on the keyboard. "Play the piano like a bongo drum for a while, with no regard for how it sounds. Just bounce around the keyboard responding to each other."

They stopped anticipating what might sound impressive, and allowed themselves to explore freely. The sound excited us most when they paid the least attention to it and focused more on their own interaction with each other. Another pair that got momentarily stuck with cautious reserve tried the same trick we had used with movement—attempting to produce only random sounds that had no connection. Allowing randomness resulted in sounds that related. When these two got past their initial skittish caution, they started having fun with each other, and we in turn had a great time listening and watching them ham it up.

By the next round of improvisations, no one needed any prodding. Each person in the group had experienced a surprising burst of energy at the piano rather than the nervousness and trepidation they had expected. About this time I started recording so they could listen to what they had done. They knew they were enjoying themselves, but they were not expecting to enjoy hearing their efforts played back to them. The fact that much of their improvising actually worked musically surprised them. They rather liked the unpremeditated, suspiciously contemporary bursts of sound, the dramatic confrontations, the uninhibited frolics that made no pretense of following a harmonic structure.

Several of them had felt selfconscious about improvising on the piano because they connected it only with improvising melodically with a structured harmonic background. Whenever they had tried this kind of improvising, they had experienced as much anxiety about mistakes as when they sight-read or performed by memory. One of the great bonuses of free improvisation is that it rescues us from any such compulsion to be accurate. One woman who found structured improvisation natural and easy discovered that when she went back after a freer approach she had gained new freshness and was aware of richer possibilities. Those starting with a free approach, later found that harmonic improvisation had lost some of its terror.

I write a great deal about how crucial it is to give ourselves permission to fail—to make mistakes—and how important it is to send our judges off temporarily on a chartered bus when we begin to experiment. Free-wheeling improvisation is a powerful tool for encouraging this sense of exploring without the shadows of our judges interfering. Without even mentioning judges, I find they slip out the back door the moment people in the group allow their sense of fun and curiosity to take over. Before that moment, the judges hang around echoing old admonitions: "Stop banging on the piano and practice your lesson," or "You're just fooling around wasting time. Now get down to business."

With judges out of the way, the group was ready to set some limitations by choosing a focal point for their improvisations, allowing internal images to flow into sounds. They started by choosing single colors to depict. It's astonishing how often a person's concept of a color can come through convincingly in an unplanned improvisation. They tried improvising with a number of other images over the next few days: a mountain storm, a moonlit beach, a noisy farmyard. They chose to portray pictures from around the room, personalities of well-known people or of those in the room. At times they chose to blow cobwebs away, to spin golden threads, or to take off on a hang glider. Their improvisations at the piano developed more depth and character when some of us began to dance what we were hearing. Watching us dance gave the pianists even more to respond to, adding to the richness of their interpretations.

The atmosphere changed once again when they added sounds from inside the piano to their repertoire: plucking individual strings for harp-like sounds, guitar-picking a silvery glissando on upper strings, using a soft mallet on the bass strings for deep-voiced resonance. They discovered a whole new world when one of them held the damper pedal down and the flutist played into the inside cavern of the grand piano.

With the dampers off, the strings picked up sympathetic vibrations and created a wonderful resonating chamber. The fading vibrations inside the piano prompted imaginative responses on the keyboard.

On another day we added the delicate shimmers from wind chimes and blew on odd-shaped wine bottles to add mystery to the sounds we were making. Someone brought in a large heavy pan lid that sounded like a gong. When we struck it and lowered it slowly into a tub of water, we got an "other-world" sound. In my studio I have a rack with varying lengths of threaded steel rods (used in construction, and available at any hardware store) that sound like chimes when struck. In another corner rests one of my favorite improvisation instruments—a piece of sheet metal three feet square. If you hold the upper edge and shake it gently you become a storm-god making thunder. As people began experimenting with such sounds, they became even more creative at the keyboard. By now the flutist and cellist felt comfortable about adding their instruments. We found that with so many sounds available we needed to make good use of silence and to tune ourselves carefully to the total collage of sound lest we destroy a delicate balance. If we got carried away with the importance of a particular instrument that any one of us was playing, we missed opportunities for the special moments that happened when we really listened. At times it felt best to limit an improvisation to only flute and cello, or cello and piano and percussion, or flute and wind chimes and inside-the-piano sounds. The possibilities were endless, and we found ourselves constantly going in new directions with new sounds.

Despite the joy we found in such improvising, one of the high points of the week occurred when we abandoned all our instruments. One person started drumming out a rhythmic tattoo on someone else's back, another person beat out a counter-rhythm on the floor and someone else's knees, a couple of us added the sound of our dancing feet to the other sounds, and before long we all added vocal sounds. The energy level in the room rose to a high pitch before that improvisation finally began winding down. We had come a long way from those first tentative attempts at improvised sound and movement.

By the time a group like this has worked together for a number of sessions, people develop a surprising amount of spontaneity and drop much of their usual selfconsciousness. I remember the day, many years ago, when I was in the midst of teaching a series of improvisation classes for piano teachers. The group surprised me that particular day, for they went from improvised singing to vocalized nonsense syllables and from there to some marvelous dialogues in pure gibberish. Remember making up your own language when you were a kid, or playing as if you were talking a foreign language with a friend? When I was young, my parents spoke German, but only on the telephone with relatives or to each other when they didn't want our long ears listening in. My sisters and I used to pretend we also knew a foreign language, and delighted in jabbering away at each other in our improvised tongue.

Back to our little circle of usually sedate piano teachers who looked anything but sedate as they rattled away, waving their arms and gesticulating and discovering their flair for drama. Talking in gibberish is something like doing mime with whiteface, or dressing up in a costume that gives us permission to act out a more vivid and vocal character than our "real-life" one. That character can shout, stamp about with perfect freedom, and later that same character can lend authenticity to a performance of a Beethoven sonata.

While we were discovering these hidden characters, a friend dropped by the studio and peeked in to see what was going on. The moment he opened the door, people became selfconscious, fell silent, and looked up with embarrassed looks. They needn't have worried. My friend was not one to miss an opportunity for a bit of drama. When I asked him—in gibberish—to join us, he walked in as though he had rehearsed his role ahead of time. The new-found characters playing hide and seek within the room dropped their concerns and welcomed the kindred spirit in my friend that leaped out, ready for action.

Improvisation, whether it be on bongo drums, in movement, in gibberish, with instruments, or whatever, has a profound effect upon us. We live our lives within narrow boundaries, often unaware of the characters waiting to peek out from behind the curtains and be recognized. The characters are not phony—they are real parts of ourselves wanting expression. Each time we give birth to one of these unsuspected parts, our lives become richer, and we open doors to a mystifying level of creativity within us. If we get too caught up with going about the business of what we think life is all about, we can become pretty stodgy and rigid. Our stodginess and rigidity can separate us from the whirling dimensions of these inner selves that yearn silently for expression. These characters beckon through the fog of everyday routine, tantalizing and frightening us at the same time. We fear being yanked out of the cloak of dull safety that we have sewed ourselves into. Yet we also welcome opportunities to do more than wave back at these other selves.

I use improvisation for many reasons. It can spark rich ideas for composition, for it gives us a more intimate sense of the raw materials of sound. It provides an astonishing physical and emotional release, and helps develop the kind of spontaneity that can transform the way we play Bach or Mozart or Bartok. It creates a more direct personal relationship with an instrument that can melt square-shouldered bravado into keen-eared listening.

Improvisation helps to free us in areas of our lives where we create imaginary boundaries that we dare not trespass. When I am free to improvise freely in my life, I shake hands with new parts of myself that sometimes startle, sometimes delight me. Whether startled or delighted, I always walk away more alive, more filled with *me* in a clean, clear way.

16.
Soprano
on
Her
Feet

A year after encountering my first "soprano on her head," I met another. This soprano had enrolled in a week-long university workshop hoping for some fresh ideas that would release some of her tension over an upcoming appearance with a symphony orchestra on the east coast. Though not on her head when I met her, she got carried away when she read a draft of my first chapter, and talked me into a similar experiment. She liked it so well on her head that I wasn't sure I could get her back on her feet!

Since a soprano obviously can't build a career standing on her head, I felt obligated to get her right-side-up again. Experimenting must ultimately lead us back to singing on our feet, or playing the piano in a bow tie, or playing a violin concerto in a proper concert where simple craziness is not highly valued.

But often we must stand on our heads before we can go back to standing on our over-taught feet. The sheer novelty shakes loose something tight and hard, leaving our brain cells free to reorganize in a new way. New ways, so refreshing at first, can in their turn become rigid, and we must be on the alert for the next appropriate session of head-standing.

It's strange what we assume about learning. How often we pretend someone must force it upon us, and that we in turn must force it upon others. We get all tangled up in concepts and instructions. Can you remember when you learned to ride a bicycle—to balance precariously on two skinny wheels? Did anyone really help by trying to explain it to you? I remember when my five-year-old son, Dan, exploded into the house with "Mommy, I hopped on Vicki's bike and rid it a smidgy—a teeny smidgy!" There were no words to mess him up, as there had been with Vicki, our first born, no parents/instructors/judges standing around to watch, and rob him of his ecstasy.

It was not the first time he had "hopped on Vicki's bike," but it was the first time he had "rid it a teeny smidgy." His joy was all the greater because of the previous times when he had landed in a heap.

When Vicki learned to ride, she didn't know the ecstasy she was being robbed of by our over-instructing. How often we are robbed of our ecstasy by trusting implicitly in external authority and negating our internal wisdom. And how often we—like Vicki—don't even *notice* that we have been robbed. We wobble along obeying the edicts from visible or invisible judges, negating the closer truth in our own bodies or minds. "Lean to the right—no, no, to the left. No! Turn your handlebars this way—no, *no*, NO!" We yield our wills and our imaginations to "experts," both visible and invisible, and pretend that only the experts have god-given powers of perception. We forget the legitimacy of our own knowing.

I relearn time and again that when I acknowledge and experience the authenticity of my own understanding—no matter how minimal that understanding might be—I can reach out more easily to touch and feel and taste and explore the perception of others. The very process of my touching and exploring, rather than gulping, transforms the expert's advice or counsel. It either melts into my own perceptions, nourishing and enriching me, or it bobbles back up to the surface, clearly unusable. If I gulp indiscriminately, I'm apt to suffer mental indigestion, for my mind can't handle all this hard-packed, dehydrated information. I remember a friend preparing for doctoral exams who said his head was so stuffed with bits and pieces of stuff labeled "knowledge" that it felt like each bit was written on a fragile strip of paper, and then tamped down solidly. He wondered whether he could extricate the right piece at the right moment when he took his exams.

What about the day I become the expert myself, the parent, the authority, the specialist, the teacher? How do I continue to believe in my own expertise, and yet keep my sense of humor about its value?

If I am ever tempted to feel complacent about my own teaching, I remember when a young friend inadvertently sparked that sense of humor. He stopped by one spring to see if I wanted to share a load of horse manure that he was collecting from nearby stables. Always eager for a little organic substance to mellow the clay in my garden, I responded enthusiastically. He turned up a few days later with the manure and asked when he could stop by to collect a piano lesson in exchange.

A deal is a deal, even after the fact, so I found time to give him the lesson. From time to time I remember with a wry grin what my wisdom is worth! Perhaps it was actually the greatest compliment I could have received, for I like the analogy of organic matter that breaks up the hard stickiness of clay soil. There's a lot of that kind of soil around, and most of it isn't in gardens. We could each use help in breaking up our own private brand of clay. We all need imagination to break down the stodginess of sterile knowledge. I like the idea of fertilizing as well— furnishing nourishment for living and growing. We all need a lot of nourishment to keep growing. All in all, it was a good trade, and one to keep me from overrating my skills.

Often we mistake knowledge for truth and forget that the sun shines on truth from different directions and casts a different shadow each time. When we look only at high noon, we miss a lot. If we mistake the shadow for truth itself, we delude ourselves. Our understanding must shine from ever-new directions.

Once in a Scrabble game I had the letters B R O I N A and a blank. By using the blank as an S and using an A already available on the board I could have made the eight-letter word "abrasion" for a modest score, with a fifty point bonus for using all seven letters. But the free A disappeared before my turn. My mind was so stuck on the word "abrasion" that I almost missed the possibility of juggling my letters one more time, using the blank as a W and making the word "rainbow." I ended up with a triple-word score on rainbow, plus forming two extra words along the way, plus my fifty point bonus for going out. It was a perfectly obvious move once I turned loose of my first word and played around with new possibilities for the blank. But the word "abrasion" was a long way from the word "rainbow." It took the juggling—the act of disorienting myself, disengaging myself from the orderliness of the first word I discovered—to find a new word. I had a sense of commitment to my first word, and a sense of loss when it disappeared from the realm of possibility that all but prevented me from going beyond it. The word "abrasion" was not wrong; it simply no longer fit the Scrabble board.

We are surrounded by orderly logical concepts that appear to fit our lives. But someone makes a move ahead of us and the concept no longer works. Or if the concept works for a friend, or a guru, or a teacher, we command it to work for us as well. When it doesn't, we tend to mistrust our own intelligence or will power rather than the concept. It seems a cop-out to take the concept apart, scramble all the elements, and see what turns up. In Scrabble, if my letters are all vowels—say, E I I I O O A—I may go farther if I choose to miss a turn for the privilege of trading my letters for a new set. There are a lot of concepts that we continue to revere without seeing them either as hopeless junk that needs trading in, or as ideas badly in need of juggling.

When my sopranos responded to head-standing, they set the stage for brain-joggling freshness. From there they had to work themselves back up to an acceptable position without losing their new insights. If they had gotten stuck with only the *fact* of the head-standing trick, they would have missed the point. The trick itself was of little consequence; the insights and new information were of the utmost significance. Neither of them found an "answer" while standing on her head, but rather a way of shaking off the crusty accumulation of habits from years of overzealous training.

I worked with Laura, a professional clarinetist who took great delight in all the tricks I came up with to break up her old rigid patterns. When she first came to me she was depressed and discouraged from working with teachers who in her words ". . . measure everything I do with a slide rule . . . stop me in the middle of a phrase because I should have had a quarter-inch bigger crescendo . . . and leave me feeling guilty, always guilty, no matter how hard I work. . . ." Laura felt that when she did play beautifully, they seldom noticed, for they were too absorbed in fly-swatting her "mistakes." This had left her so demoralized that she was terrified of an upcoming audition for a symphony job.

Experimenting in awareness was a switch for her, and she reveled in each new insight. Yet she came back session after session with her jaw locked, her lips pinched around the mouthpiece, her diaphragm like concrete, her ribs like iron braces. She would pick out a passage that was troubling her from her orchestral or solo repertoire, play it, and swear. Next would come an elaborate reed routine. (A clarinet reed is always either too hard or too soft, too heavy or too light. If you trim it to perfection, it promptly splits. The search for a perfect reed could presumably occupy a clarinetist for an entire lifetime!) Laura would flavor the reed routine with a colorful diatribe towards anyone stupid enough to take up such an impossible instrument. I wondered why she tortured herself with six to eight hours of practice each day on an instrument she apparently loathed so much.

Then—my trick. Perhaps I would ask her to breathe through the soles of her feet (impossible, of course, but when she tried, she felt grounded and forgot to get tense), or to sense the backs of her eyeballs (the sensation was so novel that she played a perfect run before she could think about its difficulty), or to sense the bore, the hollow core, of her instrument (the tone automatically became richer), to sense a bore inside her body to correspond to that in her clarinet (tone richer still), to dramatize the difficulties of a passage (which ceased to be as difficult the moment she dramatized them), or to dance or mime the character of the passage (this one never failed to make a dramatic change in her playing). Whenever a passage began to work, she would be newly surprised and incredulous. It was great fun for both of us. When she was down on herself she had a deadly, unfunny humor that she zapped herself with. But when she had been coaxed out of her half-phony cynicism by a successful experiment, her inner clowns came to the rescue, bringing moments of great clarity.

I realized, however, that we almost had to start all over again each time. When I shared this concern with her, she saw that she was becoming addicted to the drama of her rescues, whereas previously she had been addicted to the drama of humiliation. David Burge, now head of the piano department at Eastman School of Music, Rochester, N.Y., first pointed out to me the possibility of addiction to humiliation when I was voicing indignation over the authoritarian "teach by humiliation" style of a number of teachers at a summer music festival. "It's addictive, Eloise," I remember him saying. "Students hate it, but always assume they deserve it, and keep going back week after week for more." Frightening.

Neither of her addictions pleased Laura. For years she had played a totally passive role at lessons, preparing conscientiously each week, then putting herself at the mercy of an all-knowing superior who could crush her spirit for days with one bit of devastating criticism. She was still playing a comparatively passive role, even though she was now enjoying herself. I wanted her to recognize her own ability to solve problems through the help of our experiments. Instead she invested me with the power, had a great time having her problems fixed, then went home and swore again at her clarinet.

Although I hate to admit it, I suspect that I was seduced at first by my own success in helping to bring about such dramatic, on-the-spot changes in Laura's playing. She was so genuinely convinced of the insolubility of her problems and so genuinely grateful for my help that it was a new challenge to my imagination each time she came. If one of my suggestions didn't work, she took it as tangible proof of her own incompetence and lack of talent. When something *was* effective, she gave all the credit to me. It was great for my ego, and it was great for her clarinet playing—temporarily. But sooner or later she needed to start discovering her own authority rather than being convinced of my authority.

It took time. At first it was enough to discover—only in the midst of liberating experiments—the sensitive, authoritative clarinetist hiding inside. She was delighted to find the positive effects changing her in subtle ways that had nothing to do with playing the clarinet. She no longer felt the need to put herself down when she was with friends, and began regaining her natural enthusiasm for life. She had a husband who appreciated and encouraged this new growth. It took longer for the changes to filter into her professional life, for it was here that she had been the most sabotaged and felt the most vulnerable. She had to get used to the fact that she could say good-bye to the uptight, over-conscientious musician in her who had been so ready to pay homage to the superior beings of the musical world.

As she began to develop more trust in herself through her successes in my studio, she was finally able to carry the approach more and more into her own practice and to begin investigating her own rich sources of wisdom. Some real breakthroughs came when she started dreaming up experiments for her own students, thereby finding new answers for herself. It was an up-and-down process, and still is at times, but in the meantime she has had some good experiences studying with a couple of clarinetists from major symphonies who have warmly supported her new-found confidence and freedom.

The lesson was a good one for us both. It is so easy to see quick, almost instantaneous results in a workshop, that we sometimes forget what a long, difficult stretch lies ahead for anyone who embarks on the journey of awareness, on the journey of dealing with inner judges. Over and over, while writing, I have had to edit out the word "suddenly" when I describe experiments that release us from the clutches of our own self-imposed tyranny. Yet, each time, the word was astonishingly accurate. I edited it out in many places only because it is misleading. Insight *is* sudden. It is a flash of understanding. It's what we *do* with our insights that can take a lifetime.

It takes time to break old patterns—time and patience—and though "will power" may seem a forgotten/forbidden word in this book, it does take an act of will. It takes an act of will to become vulnerable enough to explore scary, unknown territory in our minds and bodies. It takes will power to keep from sliding along in the track someone else makes for us in the snow without realizing when it is time to make our own tracks. It takes will power and courage to suffer the turmoil of change.

It's far easier for any of us to go back to the old game of collecting formulas and measuring ourselves against them. Formulas give us chunks of substance to reassure ourselves with, whether in teaching or learning or enduring a crisis in the family. If we have something solid to hang on to, we need not take the step into unfamiliar territory. There is a certain amount of comfort in looking about and finding the red house on the corner, the big elm tree by the bridge, the old windmill in the pasture. Yet if we look more closely, we often find that the red paint is peeling and the house dilapidated, the familiar tree rotted with disease and ready to fall, the windmill an anachronism that stopped working in the thirties. And it's time for something new.

Yet new ideas can be as dangerous. A man I know left a semester of stimulating graduate work saying "I'm trying to figure out how to *concretize* these great new ideas." I always shudder when I hear something like this. I'm not sure what a word like "concretize" really means, but I don't like the sound or the feel of it. It smacks of new concrete which can set harder than old concrete.

Insight is different. It takes the concrete out and leaves things more fluid. Life has lots of genuine-sounding simulated answers waiting to be snatched up by gullible takers. Finding a "real" answer is as illusory as finding a "real" ending for a novel. I can still get so caught up with a good story that I can momentarily be taken in by a convincing denouement. But all endings are illusory. All solutions to problems are phony at some level, because the flip side of an ending is a new beginning; the flip side of a solution is the recognition of the next problem.

It would be nice, for instance, to say that Liz, my original soprano (on her head), lived happily ever after (on her feet), all her singing problems solved by one dramatic episode in a slightly zany workshop. But as with all real-life stories, the script got messed up. Part of it does read like a story-book, for she did find the courage to quit her teaching job the year following the workshop and move to the west coast to seriously pursue a singing career. She was *so* serious however, that it was her undoing. She immediately found a "good" voice teacher to study with, and just as immediately locked herself back into her suit of armor. Her "shoulds" and "oughts" were back again, through no fault of the teacher, and she called me in a panic. "I even tried singing on my head again, Eloise," she moaned. "And guess what? It didn't work. *It didn't work at all!*" She was afraid that she had lost whatever it was she thought she had, and at this point wasn't clear any more what it had been.

Of course it didn't work to sing on her head. Ridiculous to think it might. Back to formulas again. If it doesn't work on your feet, try singing on your head. But it doesn't work that way. Liz could sing on her head that first time because she wasn't *told* to try singing on her head. She discovered that position through following her own path of experimentation. When she arrived there, it was a position of freedom. Nothing was at stake. Her body was loose and easy from previous warm-ups and she had released her usual expectations. She was so comfortable and relaxed at that point that she might have found results as spectacular in many different positions.

Liz, now struggling to establish a career out in California, was back to trying her best, even if it meant upending herself to recapture something lost. But she took all her tension and new expectations right down to the floor with her, and was disappointed. The fact that I had taken the title for my book from her experience made those expectations more pressing. Surely if her head-standing had produced a book title she should be able to duplicate the experience at will.

We saw each other a month later when I went to California to lead some workshops. I was impressed again with her magnificent voice. "Yes, I know it's good," she said honestly, "but I could cry when I think how much better it could be if I didn't tighten up." True.

I asked her what quality she wanted in her singing, and she described beautifully the rich, effortless vibrance that she longed for. "I hate it when my voice gets shrill."

"Show us what you mean by shrill," I said. She took the bait, and the restraint dropped away. . . . "Is that what you mean by shrill?" I asked.

"Not really. I actually liked how that felt and sounded. Let me try again."

Her second attempt at shrillness sounded even better. "Oh, come on," she said. "Do you mean that if I want it to sound good, I should simply try to make it sound *bad*? Or was it just that once again you tricked me out of trying so hard to make it beautiful?"

"Could be," I said, and we found a few other places where she could put her awareness other than into her usual straining effort. I put my hands on her lower back and asked her simply to be aware of how my hands felt. I asked her to follow the vibrations of her voice around the room, to sense the space between the front of her chest and the back of her spine, to dance the music with her arms as she sang. Each experiment opened up the sound still more by taking her mind off the conscientiousness that ordinarily got in her way. "Liz, if you could sing the way you want, how would you sing? Can you act out what you want, even though the sound might not be right?" She hesitated for an instant, wondering if she would get the sound her new voice instructor in California wanted.

But Liz knew what *she* was after, and something suddenly clicked. "Suddenly" again. But it *was* suddenly and I refuse to qualify it this time. She was thirty-five years old, and she had been behaving like an eighteen-year-old going to the "singing master," pathetically eager for his approval. With a new gleam in her eye, she pulled out the famous aria from "Carmen" and opened it on the piano for her accompanist. Her eyes turned darker, and we could almost see a costume change as she became Carmen. She was running a fever that day, and should have been in bed, but she sang right through the fever and the weakness and her usual stage-fright clutch. She sang as she *wanted* to sing, as she longed to sing, as she was meant to sing. She didn't worry about expectations. She didn't *try* to sing. She just sang. *No head-standing nonsense today, thank you. I'll take mine standing up. And striding around the room. And singing from the heart, and who cares about ribs and diaphragms and resonating chambers and diction! I've got a voice and I know it and I'm delighted and I can show the whole world.*

It would be nice to end with that. A rousing performance, all was well, and they signed her up at the Met. Not quite. There have been some more telephone calls from California, some S.O.S.'s when a tough performance was coming up, some sharing of insights when it was over. But the singing engagements are beginning to come more often now, and the results are more and more reassuring. It's too early to tell for sure, but I have a feeling that my soprano on her head will take it from here—on her feet!